Two Hundred Years In

San Juan Capistrano

A Pictorial History

By
Pamela Hallan-Gibson

The Paragon Agency
Publishers
Orange, CA

Two Hundred Years In San Juan Capistrano
A Pictorial History

Hallan-Gibson, Pamela, 1944–

Published by
The Paragon Agency
Orange, California, 2005

1. San Juan Capistrano (Calif.)—Description—Views.
2. San Juan Capistrano (Calif.)—History—Pictorial works.
    I. Title.

F8695H35   979.4'96-dc20

Library of Congress Catalogue Card Number 95-78454

Two Hundred Years In San Juan Capistrano: A Pictorial History / Pamela Hallan-Gibson
p. cm.
Includes bibliographical references and index.
ISBN: 1–891030-48-5

Front cover illustration of the Great Stone Church by Richard Clinton
Back cover illustration of Mission Basilica San Juan Capistrano by Richard Clinton
Title page illustration of Dana Point by Edward Cochems, courtesy of Ron Sands

First Edition, 1990
Second Edition, 2005

1k • r2
Printed in USA

__Epigraph__

I am San Juan Capistrano,

Where soft ocean breezes whisper through sycamore leaves
and
caress the faces of evening strollers,

Where winter twilight is a handful of diamonds
flung against the sky,

And summer mornings are hillsides of golden mustard
and fields of ripening corn,

I am the smell of leather saddles and galloping horses,
orange
blossoms, eucalyptus bark, and adobe earth,

I am clouds of swallows darting under eaves, sandy
creekbeds that
swell into proud rivers during winter rains, and majestic
ridgelines sharply etched by the setting sun,

I am San Juan Capistrano,
Where progress is cradled in the arms of the past and gently
rocked into the future.

Pamela Hallan-Gibson

The San Juan Capistrano
Historical Society

Contents

Acknowledgments

Fifteen years ago San Juan Capistrano celebrated two bicentennials — its own, and the two hundredth anniversary of the United States. Bicentennial fever spurred many to write books about their local communities. This book, in its original form, was one of them.

Originally titled, Dos Cientos Anos en San Juan Capistrano, the book was first published in 1975 as a project of the San Juan Capistrano Bicentennial Committee. It was 144 pages with sixty-one pictures in a paper-covered six-by-nine-inch format.

The book was sold out many years ago and was never re-printed. This book, which is an updated, edited pictorial edition of the original, came into being through the generous sponsorship of the City of San Juan Capistrano, the San Juan Capistrano Chamber of Commerce and the San Juan Capistrano Historical Society. The name, unchanged except that it is now in English, recounts the two-hundred plus years of history and change which has taken place in this unique community. Like the original, this book is not meant to be a complete history. It is a sketch, an impression, an outline peppered with anecdotes. Since it is not footnoted, sources are provided within the text for the serious researcher who wishes to further pursue special topics. A brief bibliography is also provided for this purpose.

Fifteen years have elapsed since this book, which was my first, was written. While there were many who helped with the original project, and I heartily thank them again, I would like to acknowledge those who have been of particular assistance with the updated version: Jean Gibson, who retyped the original manuscript onto a diskette; Carolyn Adamson of First American Tide Insurance and Trust who helped locate pictures, Nick Magalousis who shared documents and information; Mike Darnold and Tom Baker who turned over their photo collections; Jennifer Williams, who coordinated the project on behalf of the city; the Historical Society Board of Directors and the San Juan Capistrano Walking Tour Guides who have supported all of my projects, and my fellow Orange County historians — dinosaurs all — who keep me humble. Special thanks to my husband Mark Gibson, my son, David Hallan and my daughter, Shelley Hallan, who provide encouragement and advice, and to my six cats — Nugget, Pest, Rodent, Bat, Vixen, and Scooby — who are so interested in history that they jump right up to the computer screen to get a better look. Finally, thanks to generations of San Juan Capistrano residents for being interesting, lively, and very special.

Pamela Hallan-Gibson
1990

Preface

*T*wo Hundred Years in San Juan Capistrano by Pamela Hallan-Gibson is a colorful tale of missionaries, pirates, bandits, and rancheros, of farmers, merchants, bootleggers, and politicians. Founded in 1776, San Juan Capistrano is the oldest settlement in Orange County. It has been part of Spain, Mexico, and the United States and each era has left its own distinct cultural flavor.

The book traces the decline and fall of Mission San Juan Capistrano and the ensuing period of Mexican domination with its flamboyant personalities and thousand-acre land grants. It follows the rise of American culture through the tumultuous period after 1850 when lawlessness was rampant and it took a disaster to bring diversified farming to the valley.

It examines the post-1900 years of progress when the sleepy little town awakened to form an identity of its own and the mission enjoyed a renaissance as the world-famous home of the swallows.

Originally this book was printed in 1990 and sponsored by the City of San Juan Capistrano, the San Juan Capistrano Chamber of Commerce, and the San Juan Capistrano Historical Society. The book was printed in hardcover in over 2000 copies, all of which have been sold. In 2004 the San Juan Capistrano Historical Society felt that this book should be reproduced as more and more people have requested copies. Only this time it is in soft-cover. The Society has borne the total cost of publishing this second edition. It is without doubt the most substantive book ever written about this city's rich history. The original text has basically remained intact even though many changes have occurred in this city since the original publication. Many photos that were in the original, regrettably have been lost or unavailable and these have been substituted with photos of equal quality and interest. In a few cases and to assist the reader as to current location, changes in the caption text have been updated.

It is the policy and responsibility of this historical society to keep the public aware of the unique history of Orange County's oldest community. At the Society's headquarters in the O'Neill Museum located at 31831 Los Rios Street, is this city's treasure trove of resources on San Juan Capistrano's history. Housed here are over 6000 historic photos, files of information and documents, oral histories, genealogical records, a small library of local and California history, video tapes, old newspapers, and much more for researchers.

We want to take this opportunity to thank Richard Clinton, a local professional photographer, for the two exceptional photos on the cover of this book. The front cover is a current photo of the Mission San Juan Capistrano forecourt showing part of the Great Stone Church, Companario, and the Father Serra and Indian boy statue. The back cover is the new Mission Basilica San Juan Capistrano located on the corner of Camino Capistrano and Acjachema Street behind the Mission grounds.

Also, our thanks to Ron Sands for allowing us to use part of his panoramic photo of Dana Point and the cove. This photo was taken by his uncle around 1920. It was here that Richard Henry Dana, author of "Two Years Before the Mast", noted that, "San Juan is the only romantic spot on the coast..." The inclusion of this photo represents a locale that was an integral part of San Juan Capistrano history.

A special thanks also to Doug Westfall, publisher of The Paragon Agency, and his wife Jackie, who worked with us tirelessly in reproducing this book, cost-effectively and attractively, for the benefit of our readers.

And last, but not least, we give our most heartfelt thanks to Pamela Hallan-Gibson for permitting us to reproduce her book with the changes we have noted and without any remuneration to her. All profits will go to the benefit of the Society.

"Preserving the past to enhance the future"

The Board of Directors
San Juan Capistrano Historical Society

The mission is pictured here as it appears during the height of its prosperity, around 1811,
from a painting by Lloyd Harting.
Courtesy of the San Juan Capistrano Historical Society

Chapter 1

Mission Halcyon Days 1776 – 1821

Most people, thanks to an old song and a flock of punctual birds, have heard of San Juan Capistrano. It can be found in magazines, history books, novels, movies, and an occasional television commercial. Bumper stickers say "follow the swallows to Capistrano" and T-shirts quip "Capistrano is for the birds." Thousands of people visit the community each year, drawn by Mission San Juan Capistrano with its atmosphere of old Spain, its tame pigeons, and well-tended gardens. Blood red bougainvillea spills over the ruined arches of the Great Stone Church, destroyed in the earthquake of 1812. Fat goldfish swim in serene fountains. Footsteps echo on uneven walkways that once felt the bare feet of Indians, the sandaled feet of friars, and the heavy boots of conquistadors.

A drop of rain, tracing a pattern down an adobe wall, can, in time, become a river carving a channel through a mud-clay structure until nothing is left. But Mission San Juan Capistrano has survived the rains of dos cientos anos — two hundred years — and has given the city that grew around it a special legacy: an example of stoic endurance, a unique architectural influence, a basis for the city's major industry, tourism, and a rich cultural heritage that spans two centuries.

In October of 1776, on the other side of the continent, George Washington's pleas for the creation of a national army were finally heeded by government leaders and the Revolutionary War, which would establish the United States of America, took a new direction. On the West Coast a handful of Indians, a small detachment of soldiers, and two Franciscan priests dug the pits for mixing mud and reeds that would fashion the first structures of Mission San Juan Capistrano. The activities in the East were not unknown to the settlers in the West. A scribbled note on the margin of an old book discovered in the mission in 1931 said, "I have this day prayed for the success at arms of Mr. George Washington whose cause seems to be just." Mission padres were asked to offer more than their prayers. According to historian Henry Panian of Orange Coast College, the Capistrano mission received word in August of 1781 from King Carlos III that it was to contribute funds to the American cause. Monterey sent the largest contribution, $833, and though it had only been in existence for five years, Mission San Juan Capistrano managed to send $229. Unfortunately the funds, sent via Spain, did not reach the Americans until after the surrender of Cornwallis in October of 1781.

The story of San Juan is as old as the United States and, like its foster parent, it begins earlier than 1776. It begins with a contingent of foot soldiers blazing a trail from San Diego northward in search of Monterey Bay in 1769. These men were part of the 62-man expedition led by Gaspar de Portolá. They trudged through the golden hills of Southern California in summer, noting potential mission sites and assessing the Indians who dwelled in the valleys and gawked at the unusual looking strangers. They were a lusty, fearless group in their thick leather vests, made to withstand the thrust of an Indian's arrow, and because of their attire they were called "the leather jackets." Noted California historian Hubert Howe Bancroft described the men of Portolá as the "cream of the crop," some of Spain's finest sons. Among that group were Jose

King Carlos III of Spain was in power when Mission San Juan Capistrano was founded. Courtesy of the Spanish Consulate, Los Angeles

valleys we found a village of heathen who, as soon as they saw us, began to shout and they came out as if to meet us at the watering place where we went to stop."

The Indians were friendly and excited, staring openly at the marchers. A few were frightened, hanging back as though sensing the changes that the strangers would bring. After a short walk, Father Crespi described his first glimpse of what would become the Capistrano Valley, though he had already given this name to another and would call this valley after another saint:

"A little before eleven we came to a very pleasant green valley, full of willows, alders and live oaks and other trees not known to us. It has a large arroyo, which at the point where we crossed it, carried a good stream of fresh and good water, which, after running a little way, formed into pools in some large patches of tules. We halted there, calling it the valley of Santa Maria Magdalena."

This valley, as others, was dotted with Indian rancherias, or settlements. Father Crespi described the Indians of the area as cautious, friendly and curious. The Indians of the Capistrano Valley belonged to a tribe that occupied a triangular territory from Las Pulgas Creek in the Oceanside area, northeast to the hilltops above Lake Elsinore, northwest to Saddleback Mountain, and west along Aliso Creek to the Pacific Ocean. Believed to be of Shoshone stock because of cultural similarities, local historians have given the Indians various names. Two of the most popular, Ahachmai and Acagchemem, may have been names associated with the places where they lived. Today the Indians are called Juaneño, a name adapted from Juan in San Juan Capistrano.

Indian life was described by one of the early Franciscans assigned to San Juan, Father Geronimo Boscana. In his manuscript, *Chinigchinich* he told

Antonio Yorba and Francisco Serrano, whose heirs would settle Orange County and become some of its leading citizens.

The expedition marched into what is today Orange County in late July, camping near the then-future mission site on July 23. Father Juan Crespi, who kept a diary of the journey, wrote about baptizing two Indian children in the vicinity of San Clemente and then described the rest of the morning's walk:

"We passed two valleys with dry arroyos both grown with alders and large live oaks. In one of the

The first Orange County area baptism took place in 1769 during the Portola Expedition in the San Clemente area.
Courtesy of the First American Title Insurance Company

about the beliefs, customs, and daily life of the Indians. Some early historians wrongly characterized the Indians of the area as being simple, lazy, and dull. They called them "digger" Indians and shrugged them off as unworthy of study. Father Boscana's manuscript shows us a different picture. Although he did not approve of the Indians' way of life and tended to judge them by European standards, he still provides one of the best pictures of life in the valley at the time of the coming of the Spaniards.

One anthropologist who used Boscana's information was A. L. Kroeber, one of the foremost authorities on California Indians. Kroeber described the Juaneños as having an organized, ritualistic society which included worship of a supreme deity and called for adherence to a strict cultural pattern. There were rules governing courtship, marriage, food distribution, and warfare, and there was a strict and exceedingly harsh ritual for children entering

adulthood.

Children were first given jimpson weed, which is a narcotic and stimulant. They were then expected to hallucinate and see an animal which would become their protector. It was usually a coyote, bear, rattlesnake, crow, or raven. Boys were then blistered with fire, whipped with nettles, and laid on ant hills. During this period boys were not allowed to eat meat or seeds. The girls, after being given the narcotic, were laid on branches in an earthen pit lined with heated stones and each girl was expected to fast while women with their faces painted, chanted and danced around them. The girls were often tattooed.

Special rituals were held in a ceremonial chamber, an enclosure of brush with an opening to the sky. Nearby was a coyote skin filled with feathers, horns, claws, beaks, parts of a condor, and arrows. This represented Chinigchinich, the supreme deity. A sand painting was usually placed in front of the

Father Geronimo Boscana wrote Chinigchinich, which describes the traditions of the Juaneño Indians.

Courtesy of the Southwest Museum

Missionaries are shown here in traditional eighteenth century garb. Franciscans were generally scholars, but many came with Serra to the new world to be missionaries.

Courtesy of the First American Title Insurance Company

skin. Ritual dress for those participating in the ceremony consisted of a skirt of eagle or condor feathers which hung from the waist to the knees. The headdress was a pad or wig with feathers standing upright. The body was sometimes painted with red, black, or white marks.

Father Boscana mentioned that the Juaneños had a reverence for birds, particularly condors, which they "rear from the nest with the greatest care." Birds figure prominently in their story of creation which began with the marriage of earth and sky. Out of this union came sand, rocks, flints for arrows, trees and shrubs, water, grass, and animals. One day Chinigchinich came out of the sky and created man out of clay. They believed him omniscient and worshipped him from that time.

Part of the Indian mythology, handed down from generation to generation, was a story about how they came to inhabit the valley. In a village north of San Juan dwelled a chief called Oyaison and his wife, Sirorum. After the death of his wife, the chief and his daughter, Korone, and their people went south to Niwiti, not far from San Juan. The newcomers spread out and settlements were established. One night Korone, who was exceedingly fat, swelled so much that she turned into a small hill which remains today, according to the legend. The place was called Putuidem.

This legend points up the probable migration of the Juaneños from the land of the Gabrielinos, an event which anthropologists have long

Linoleum cut prints such as this figure appeared in the Fine Arts Press 1933 edition of Chinigchinich. The book, with the color prints, was republished by the Malki Museum Press in 2005.
Courtesy of Malki Museum, Banning, CA

suspected. The village of Putuidem is believed by one anthropologist to have been located at the site of the Livingston-Graham sand and gravel pits at the east end of Trabuco Creek Road. Because of the large number of artifacts recovered from the area during the last fifty years, the spot could indeed have been the site of a large Indian habitation.

There is still much to be learned about the Juaneños from the Capistrano Valley. The discovery of artifacts and early descriptions of the valley's first residents will help complete the picture in the future. One such clue was found by historian Terry Stephenson in the 1940s:

"More mysterious and unexplainable, holding more in the way of conjecture, is another boulder upon which are pitted crude figures and an intricate maze. This rock, located on a ridge between Bell and the lower Trabuco Canyons, may be the key to the story of prehistoric occupation of California. Oldtimers have named it the Indian Mystic Rock." The rock, which is now located at Bowers Museum in Santa Ana, is an interesting remnant of Indian life in the Capistrano Valley.

Spaniards did not return to the land of the Juaneños until 1775 when Father Junipero Serra, the Franciscan in charge of setting up California's mission chain, was allowed to found another. The next site on Serra's list was San Buenaventura, but unlike the Juaneños, the Indians there were unpredictable and the padres would need a heavy guard. Reluctant to release so many soldiers at one time, the military commander talked Serra into postponing development of the San Buenaventura site. Plans were hastily changed and the next mission, the seventh in the alta California chain, became San Juan Capistrano.

Father Serra appointed Fathers Fermin Francisco de Lasuen and Gregorio Amurrio to found the new mission which would be named for an Italian

F. Swinton.

Here is an artist's conception of a Juaneño Indian in tobet, or skirt of feathers, from the Fine Arts Press 1933 edition of Chinigchinich. Courtesy of Malki Museum, Banning, CA

saint, St. John of Capistrano. Father Serra admired this saint, a member of his order, who had been canonized after fighting in the siege of Belgrade in June of 1456.

Fathers Lasuen and Amurrio both journeyed as far as Mission San Gabriel, having started from Monterey, but only Lasuen went on to San Diego to pick up supplies. Lt. José Francisco de Ortega who would help him explore the area and select the exact site of the new mission. Once this task was accomplished, they returned to San Diego, sent a letter to Amurrio, and once again set out for Capistrano. Wrote Father Francisco Palou, Serra's friend and biographer, "They took possession of the site and made a beginning of the new mission on the 30th of October, the last day of the Octave of St. John of Capistrano, patron of that mission with manifestations of pleasure from the heathen natives of that place who were present at its founding."

Construction was begun with the help of friendly Indians and the grudging help of some of the soldiers. Father Lasuen wrote later that the soldiers had not wanted to dirty their hands with construction and stressed that the padres had not forced them to assist.

"Ours was a good location near the stream La Quema (the fire) and three quarters of a league from El Camino Real in the direction of the coast," wrote Lasuen. He barely had time to lay out the proposed buildings when news arrived that on November 6, Indians had again attacked San Diego. Ortega immediately left and urged the padres to do the same. Because Father Amurrio had arrived the same day as the courier from San Diego, the mission bells were buried and everyone headed back to San Diego.

"We had just completed seven or eight days work in that place," wrote a disappointed Father Lasuen. "We had erected the mission cross, enclosed a spacious corral, mapped out the building, dug the holes in which to insert the poles, transported the lumber and gathered a large quantity of tules."

It wasn't until September 29, 1776, that governing authorities gave Father Serra permission

An Indian maze stone discovered in the Santa Ana Mountains is now on display at Bowers Museum in Santa Ana.
Courtesy of the Charles W. Bowers Museum

Father Junipero Serra was founder of the
Franciscan Missions of California.
Courtesy of the San Juan Capistrano Historical Society

settlements and teaching them to be self-sufficient according to European standards. Indians, enticed by food and glass beads, were told of the benefits of becoming part of the mission community by Indians from Mission San Gabriel. Conversion to Christianity was to be voluntary, but once converted the Indian was bound to the mission and his life controlled by the padres. He was told where to live, where to work, and what to eat. If he misbehaved, he was punished. If he ran away, he was brought back. This level of control was deemed necessary by Serra who believed the Indians needed to learn skills if they were to survive. Founding missions was only one aspect of a coordinated process used by Spanish colonizers for centuries. Concurrent with the establishment of missions was the founding of towns and military installations. Change was coming and Serra wanted the Indians to be prepared.

An additional facet of the Spanish process was that all land attached to the mission was to be held in trust for the Indians who, when ready, would take over its ownership. The entire process, which would end with the secularization of the mission, was supposed to take ten years. The enormity of the task was underestimated. Two padres were supposed to teach Christianity, farming, and a number of trades to two thousand Indians. On the other hand, Indians who had lived in a particular pattern for thousands of years were supposed to cast off their old culture and live in a completely alien way, one that was often hard to understand. The culture shock was too great; the transition too difficult.

Instead of assimilation, the Indians' right to live according to an age-old cultural pattern was forfeited as the dominant Spanish culture took its place. According to Monsignor Francis J. Weber, noted California historian, the Franciscans had often opposed premature colonization, fearing the Indians would be in jeopardy. The missions, they had hoped, would be allowed enough time to be successful

to again try to establish the Capistrano mission. This time ten soldiers and Father Pablo Mugartegui were sent with Father Amurrio back to the site. Lasuen had another assignment.

Palou wrote in his biography of Father Serra, "They arrived at the place where they found the cross still standing; they dug up the bells which had been buried and hung them for service. At the ringing of them the Indians flocked in, rejoicing to see that the Fathers had returned to their land."

On November 1, 1776, Father Junipero Serra, himself, officially founded Mission San Juan Capistrano.

What did founding a mission entail? The Franciscans were charged with gathering Indians into

Mission San Juan Capistrano

The words of the Founding Document of Mission. The original was written by Junipero Serra as a guide to assist missionaries during the mission's early years.
Courtesy of the San Juan Capistrano Historical Society

transitional tools in which Indians would be taught to survive in a Spanish culture. But ten years was not enough time, nor would fifty be.

In the new Mission San Juan Capistrano, the first order of business was obtaining supplies and constructing buildings. Father Serra himself went to San Gabriel to bring back supplies and workmen. During this trip he nearly lost his life. While riding ahead of the pack train, he and a few companions were surrounded by hostile Indians. They spared him only because a neophyte traveling with him told them that a group of soldiers rode a few leagues behind. According to Serra, this was his closest call in his years in California.

When the caravan arrived the work began. According to the founding document of Mission San Juan Capistrano, the caravan contained approximately the following: nine milk cows, a breed bull, a yoke of oxen, eight pack mules, three saddle mules, three broken horses, two mares, one colt, a male and female pig, chickens, saddles and bridles, twelve hoes, two axes, six large machetes, six new knives, a branding iron, articles for the church, and some initial food for the workers.

Where did the first construction take place? Was it at the current location or was it somewhere else? Edith Buckland Webb in *Indian Life at the Old Missions* noted that missions were occasionally moved, usually to improve the source of water. Mission fathers, as early as 1827, mentioned a mission vieja (old mission), though the exact location was never pinpointed. The most noted authority on Mission San Juan Capistrano was Father Zephyrin Engelhardt, who

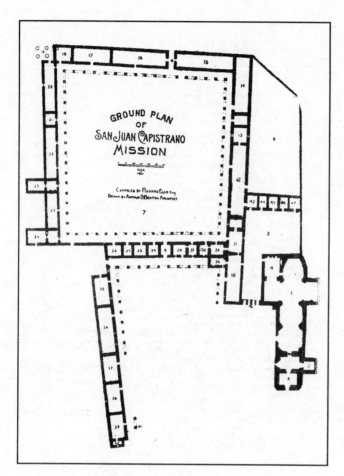

Here is a drawing of the mission as it appeared around 1806 at completion of the Great Stone Church. Courtesy of the First American Title Insurance Company

Mission San Juan Capistrano, missing for over one hundred years, were found for the years between 1779 and 1795. In the report for 1782 Father Mugartegui wrote:

"This mission was founded Nov. 1, 1776 but because of water failure at the place where it was first founded, the site was transferred to that which it occupies today, where we have the advantage of secure water. It is located about three fourths of a league (about two miles) distant from the original site. This transfer was made on October 4, 1778." He said another interesting thing: the original site was less than half way between the current site and the ocean, a location which supports Palou's description exactly.

Modern historians have placed the original site in other locations. Several accounts designated an adobe ruin five miles east of San Juan off the Ortega Highway as the mission vieja, even before it had been proven that the mission was moved. C. E. Roberts, author of the Works Progress Administration report *Adobes of Orange County*, published in 1936, visited the mission vieja site and said it contained the ruins of an adobe whose generous dimensions and tile roof would seem to confirm the opinion that it was an original mission building, though he lamented that only rubble and fragments of tiles were left.

"Early travel from the Capistrano Mission to San Luis Rey ascended the north side of San Juan Creek some five miles and then turned southward toward Cristianitos Canyon. At the mouth of the Gobernadora Canyon the road passed the adobe ranch house called the Mission Vieja." Roberts added that the dwelling had been used by sheepmen before it crumbled.

Orange County historian Don Meadows placed the location in yet another spot in 1967. He believed the old mission to be about one mile southeast of its present site at the Jean Lacouague Ranch. This site is near San Juan Creek and it is about three-fourths of a league distant from the old road. There is also evidence to suggest it was once the site of an Indian village. But there is still the conflicting data given by Palou and Mugartegui which states that the original site was halfway between the current site and the ocean, something the Lacouague Ranch is not.

Were there any ruins found near the ocean?

published a book on the mission in 1922. Father Engelhardt, in an appendix to his book, *San Juan Capistrano Mission*, explored the subject in detail and concluded that the mission was never moved. He cited Palou's description of the first site and believed it adequately described the current site:

"The site of the mission is a beautiful one with a fine view from the houses out over the sea only half a league distant from shore with good anchorage even for frigates and defended from weather during that part of the season when the vessels visit this coast...."

Engelhardt does not, however, explain why Palou says "half a league" when the distance is actually a full league and more. In 1965, Father Maynard Geiger, curator of the Santa Barbara Mission Archives and an authority on Father Serra, noted an important discovery which he made in the National Museum of Mexico. Annual reports from

Two early accounts mentioned ruins found near the sea. One was an early guidebook and the other a booklet published in 1939 called *History of Orange County* by Don Hart. Neither thought they were the mission ruins because both believed in the site five miles to the east. The location of the ruins was not given. E. L. Howell in his book, *Little Chapters about San Juan Capistrano*, which was revised from a 1912 book by the same name written by Father St. John O'Sullivan, described what he believed to be the exact location of the original cross erected by Father Lasuen in 1775. He noted it was on the grounds of the present mission.

"The site was marked by a large oval stone embedded in the ground for many years," wrote Howell in his 1949 adaptation. "It has disappeared in the last 10 years, probably moved by a gardener working in the grounds not knowing what it was placed there for." He said the stone was shown to Father St. John O'Sullivan by Acu, an Indian of the mission whose father had shown it to him.

Another piece of evidence concerning a move comes from Father Serra. In October of 1778 (the date of the move quoted by Father Mugartegui) Father Serra wrote in his personal register that he had confirmed fifty-seven neophytes in the "new mission of the same San Juan Capistrano de Quanis Savit."

The final evidence as to location comes from Father Pedro Font, chaplain of the Col. Juan B. Anza expedition, who encountered the unfinished buildings of the mission on February 8, 1776. He noted then that after crossing Trabuco Creek (moving southwest) they came to another river which they called the Arroyo de Santa Maria Magdalena (San

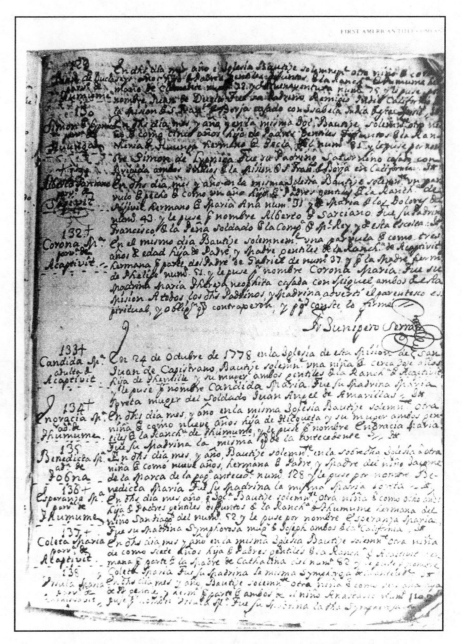

A page from the Mission Baptismal, Marriage and Death records, where all important events were recorded, is shown here.
Courtesy of the First American Title Insurance Company

Juan Creek). Between this and the ocean were unfinished structures, abandoned because of the revolt which took everyone back to San Diego.

One can safely conclude that the mission was moved from its original site to its present site, but further study is needed to pinpoint the original location (or locations). Father Mugartegui does not say the move was made because of water shortage, the usual reason for such moves, but water failure.

RIOS ADOBE

Rios Adobe was one of forty adobes built in 1794. Its first occupant was Feliciano Rios, once a soldier at the mission.
Courtesy of the San Juan Capistrano Historical Society

While it can be argued that the two terms can by synonymous, Fathers Jose Maria de Zalvidea and Josef Barona in their 1827 inventory, provide another alternative. Discussing problems with land, the report stated:

"The floods it is that cause the damage; and they have done more damage than the mustard plant. Some of the floods come from the interior; others are from the sea and run across the surface of the land." Perhaps the sea which flooded the land also affected the quality of the fresh water in the stream nearest the first site, causing water failure. This is only a theory, yet one which warrants examination.

Many questions remain unanswered. What evidence promoted the Ortega site as the mission vieja? Why was a move not mentioned in the mission's baptismal, marriage, and death books where many events affecting the mission were written? Were these ruins nearer to the sea and were these ruins what Richard Henry Dana saw when in *Two Years Before the Mast* he wrote that he could see the mission from the ocean? The mystery remains.

According to a letter written by Father Mugartegui to Father Serra, the first structures built at the new site were a church, living quarters, and a shed for calves. The first crops planted were vineyards and a vegetable garden. Father Maynard Geiger, in an article in the *Southern California Historical Quarterly* noted that the annual report for 1782–1783 confirmed that the temporary church was outside the mission quadrangle, serving until the structure known as Father Serra's Chapel could be built. It was half an adobe in thickness and supposedly served as the church from 1778 to 1782.

Some historians thought the Montanez adobe, west of the mission quadrangle, might have been this early structure. But evidence uncovered in an archaeological dig in 1974 found that the original two rooms were too wide and the adobe walls too thick to fit these dimensions. An adobe foundation south of the mission entrance, mapped by C. E. Roberts in 1936, roughly fit the dimensions, and contained the thin bricks characteristic of early construction, but it was long ago destroyed and the site has contained various buildings over the years. An examination of the foundations uncovered during the construction of the Franciscan Plaza in 1989 did not enhance this theory.

The best theory is that the structure was built on the outside edge of the quadrangle and was the building we refer to as Father Serra's Chapel. According to Father Engelhardt, this building was not erected all at one time. Father Serra supposedly complained that the building was too small, so it was enlarged. It was changed again in the 1920s to the dimensions it has today. Current studies have dated portions of the chapel to 1778, the rear portion being the oldest.

As the mission grew and prospered, so did the problems. Mrs. Fremont Older, author of the 1915 publication, *California Missions and Their Romances*, wrote about a problem concerning one of the outlying mission settlements, called rancherias: "San Juan Capistrano met obstacles usually attending young establishments: the Aloucuachomi Rancheria threatened neophytes in June, 1777; Corporal Mariano Carrillo killed three and wounded four of the offenders; a chieftain was punished for furnishing women to the Spanish guard." The missionaries seemed to have a great deal of trouble restraining the sexual proclivities of the soldiers assigned to protect them. As early as three weeks after the mission was established problems of this

nature began to develop. Father Engelhardt, who had a low opinion of mission guards, called them the worst impediment to the mission system.

"Recruited from the scum of society in Mexico, frequently convicts and jailbirds, it is not surprising that the mission guards, leather-jacket soldiers, as they were called, should be guilty of such and similar crimes at nearly all the missions. It does amaze, however, that such a scandal could happen within three weeks of the founding of the Mission, and that the presence of the Father President himself failed to check the criminal propensities of a member of the guard. Father Serra's feelings may be imagined. In truth, the guards counted among the worst obstacles to missionary progress. The wonder is, that the missionaries, nevertheless, succeeded so well in attracting converts."

Attracting converts, of course, was the principle task of the missionaries. According to Father Palou, the job was easier at San Juan. "Unlike the Indians at other missions, as the fathers wrote to me in the beginning, who would molest the missionaries by begging eatables and other presents, these of San Juan Capistrano molested the missionaries with petitions for baptism...." By 1786, ten years after the mission's founding, there were 544 Indian neophytes. Ten years after that the number had risen to 994, with 1,649 having been baptized. Although some Indians were housed on nearby rancherias, many lived in the mission

Here is the earliest drawing of San Juan Capistrano done by artist Miller in 1865.
Avila Adobe is believed to be the building at left.
Courtesy of the City of San Juan Capistrano

compound or near it. Housing was a problem, one that was attacked in 1794.

"In 1794 two granaries were built at Mission San Juan Capistrano, one measuring 34 varas or about 94 feet in length, five varas or 14 feet in width while the other was 20 varas or 55 feet in length and five varas in width. Likewise, 40 little cabins were put up for as many neophyte families. The dimensions of these dwellings were not given, but they were of adobe and some of them, like the granaries, were roofed with tiles, while others were still covered with tules until tiles could be made." Father Engelhardt found this description in a group of documents filed in the United States Land Office in San Francisco in 1904, two years before the earthquake and conflagration destroyed it. The report documented a flurry of building activity. Yet the most important structure was begun three years after the granaries and adobe homes were built. Fathers Vicente Fuster and Juan Norberto de Santiago began the construction of the Great Stone Church in 1797. The imposing edifice was to be built in the shape of a Latin cross, 180 feet long

Hippolyte Bouchard, who raided the coast of California in 1818 under the flag of Argentina, stopped in San Juan Capistrano and demanded supplies.

Courtesy of the Jim Sleeper Collection

with a 120-foot belltower at the southern end. The roof would contain six domes of masonry (some accounts say seven). Isidro Aguilar, a master mason originally from Culiacan, Mexico, was hired to supervise the work of the local neophyte workmen and the construction was begun just before spring.

Father Norberto de Santiago is usually credited with laying out the buildings that would form the nucleus of the mission village. Building wasn't a problem, but finding suitable materials sometimes was. Sandstone had to be quarried six miles away to the northeast; limestone was obtained near El Toro; sycamore wood came from Trabuco. Stones were also brought from the old mission site and from a rocky point near the ocean. Some were carried while others were brought to the mission in small wooden carts called carretas. The church gradually took form, year by year until nine years later it stood complete, a monument to the toil of the men, women, and children who helped build it. Unfortunately, Isidro Aguilar wasn't there to bask in the praise. He had died in 1803, a few years before the church was completed. The new edifice was dedicated on September 7, 1806, in the presence of many dignitaries. According to Mrs. Fremont Older, "Governor Jose Arrillaga arrived for the dedication. With him were San Diego and Santa Barbara soldiers in glittering uniforms. Neophytes from distant rancherias crowded the church. A fiesta followed which became a legend in Southern California."

The feasting and praying took several days. The church itself stood only six years for on December 8, 1812, a massive earthquake shook Southern California and the masterpiece of construction toppled to the ground. Mrs. Older pictured the event this way:

"On a summer-like morning, Dec. 8, 1812, mass was being celebrated. What was that distant roar? Was it the sea? The tower tottered. Several persons left. Father Suner and Barona were in the sacristy. People fled to the side door. Again the tower tottered. The father and neophytes escaped to the sacristy. Bells swayed, tolled, were silenced and crashed to the earth. With them fell two Indian bell ringers. The door had been twisted by the earthquake and could not be unlocked. Nearly forty neophytes were buried under the stone and mortar of the fallen tower."

One woman was found alive under the rubble, but the others perished, making the death toll thirty-nine. Another woman, found two months later, moved the toll back to forty. The building, which was thought to have been top heavy, has never been restored.

A romantic legend, found in several books and produced as a play, tells the story of two lovers, an Indian artist named Teofilo, and a half-breed girl called Magdalena. They were forbidden to marry. Magdalena rebelled and was ordered to carry a penitent's candle in front of the Indian women on the day of the earthquake. When the church began to topple, Teofilo ran to her side and both perished. The lovers are, the legend says, preserved in faded frescoes somewhere in the mission grounds, and Magdalena's face, outlined by the light of a flickering candle, can sometimes be seen in a high window of the Great Stone Church ruins.

The church was destroyed, but the mission survived. With nearly fourteen hundred people living and working in and around it, the mission was like a little city, self-contained and self-sufficient. People raised their own food, made their own clothing, and worked at many trades. The Indians were taught candlemaking, weaving, tanning of hides, soapmaking, and the fashioning of harnesses and shoes. Much of the instruction was held outside in the main quadrangle. According to Monsignor Weber, a Catholic historian, the Indians' schedule was far from arduous. The day began at sunrise with the ringing of the first bell. The second bell called the Indians to Mass, after which they had breakfast and then assembled in the courtyard for their daily tasks. The work day began at 9:00 a.m. ending at 11:15 a.m. for an hour and a half of lunch. Then another two hours of work followed. After dinner there were often games, music, and fun. The last bell was rung at 8:00 p.m. notifying everyone that the mission gates would close for the night forty-five minutes later. The day described by Monsignor Weber was, of course, an ideal day. Field and cattle hands probably followed a different schedule and work hours undoubtedly changed, depending on tasks.

In 1807 thirty-four adobes were built or remodeled. Records provided by Engelhardt showed that 1811, however, was the mission's most prosperous year. The mission produced 500,000 pounds of wheat; 190,000 pounds of barley; 202,000 pounds of corn; 20,600 pounds of beans; 14,000 cattle; 16,000 sheep; and 740 horses.

Sometimes stores were lost through tomfoolery. In March of 1801 a fire destroyed 12,500 pounds of tallow and 1,000 bushels of corn and wheat. Engelhardt noted that the fire was caused by a young boy who had entered the storeroom with a lighted candle and had "amused himself by killing bats."

Because of plentiful supplies, ships frequently stopped at the mission, anchored in the cove and men rowed to shore. Some came for supplies while others came to trade "luxury" items for mission hides and tallow. Although the missions were self-sufficient enough to raise their own food and clothing, they still depended on outsiders for specialty items — books, bells, some utensils, simple ornaments for the church, and news. Not all the visitors were welcome. Father Engelhardt described in detail the visit of a debauched officer of the ship Activo who was caught in the act of seducing a young Indian girl. The officer, forbidden by the padres to set foot on Capistrano soil again, complained to the authorities that he had been mistreated at the mission. The matter was investigated and the mission exonerated.

One of the most notorious and least welcome of San Juan's visitors came in the winter of 1818. His visit was short, his deeds not exactly nefarious. Yet his impact on the folklore of San Juan Capistrano has never been paralleled. His name was Hippolyte Bouchard, and he's known as the "pirate."

Bouchard, whose real name was Andre Paul according to Orange County historian Jim Sleeper, was not a pirate. He was a privateer, commander of two ships that raided the coast of California on behalf of the United Provinces of Rio de la Plata (Argentina). The provinces had declared independence from Spain and were technically at war. California was a Spanish colony, ripe for plunder. One of the towns he

Here are the ruins of the Great Stone Church after an earthquake destroyed it in 1812.
It stood only six years after its 1806 completion.
Courtesy of the San Juan Capistrano Historical Society

raided was Santa Barbara. After he left, messengers were sent along the coast to warn the missions of his coming. The padres moved swiftly, packing the mission valuables and transporting them and the townspeople to the Trabuco rancheria, while a small group remained to defend the town.

Bouchard's ships sailed into the harbor in December. He immediately sent sailors ashore, but these men didn't charge into town with patches over their eyes and daggers between their teeth. They marched in with a flag of truce and a message that the town would be spared if supplies would be provided. Santiago Arguello, who was in charge of the town's defense, read the message skeptically. They were, after all, enemies of Spain.

Arguello's decision was swift and final. He told them to land if they pleased, but not to expect a warm welcome. The answer enraged Bouchard who was badly in need of supplies. The next day the sailors raided the town. Peter Corney, commander of one of the ships, noted that the raiders — 140

strong with two cannons — were met by Spanish horsemen who fired a couple of shots then fled, leaving the town to be plundered. This account was supported by Juan Avila who recounted that his father, Don Antonio Ignacio Avila, had come all the way from Los Angeles to help protect the town. Putting himself in the hands of Arguello, he was dismayed when the young man gave orders to flee to the high hill behind the mission and stay there until the privateers left.

They left the next morning, but not without difficulty. Corney's account, which appeared in his *Early Voyages in the North Pacific*, was as follows:

"We found the town well stocked with everything but money and destroyed much wine and spirits and all the public property, set fire to the king's stores, barracks and governor's house and about two o'clock we marched back though not in the order that we went, many of the men being intoxicated, and some were so much so that we had to lash them to the field pieces and drag them to the beach where about six o'clock we arrived with

Documents found in the old mission date back two centuries.
Courtesy of the First American Title Insurance Company

the loss of six men. Next morning we punished about 20 men for getting drunk."

The six men lost apparently didn't die, but merely made use of the opportunity to jump ship. Historian Jim Sleeper claims that among those who did not return to the ship were Orange County's first white settler and first black.

The Bouchard incident, which most accounts exaggerate, had a lasting effect on San Juan's history because it was from then on that stories of buried treasure emerge. Some historians believe the only valuables the padres had to hide were candlesticks and altar cloths and Holy utensils. They point out that despite the mission's prosperity, Franciscans were sworn to an oath of poverty. Yet stories of treasure, still buried from the Bouchard invasion, persist to this day.

San Juan Capistrano settled back into its routine existence after Bouchard's visit. Records show that the mission had already passed its pinnacle of prosperity. Conversions were fewer, harvests down. Yet the land remained, stretching endlessly over the horizon, its sinuous contours making silent promises of abundance to come. The mission's greatest wealth was not gold, jewelled ornaments, or silver chalices. It was land.

The land assigned to Mission San Juan Capistrano under the Recopilacion de Leyes de los Reynos de las Indias covered Southern Orange County. It included land which would one day become parts of Mexican land grants, in addition to portions which would one day be granted by the Spanish Crown to Jose Antonio Yorba and Juan Pablo Grijalva, called Rancho Santiago de Santa Ana. The land extended from the Santa Ana River to San Mateo Creek and from the ocean to the top of the Santa Ana Mountains.

Franciscans considered the land held in trust for the Indians. But they waited too long to turn it over to them. Most historians agree that these vast tracts of land, coveted by man, greatly contributed to the decline of the mission system. Only one land grant was made in Orange County under Spanish rule. But with Mexican independence would come enforced secularization of the missions, and the gradual takeover of mission lands. The Indians, with one culture suppressed and the other not yet fully developed, would be the victims of the coming struggle.

It was the end of an era and the end of a way of life. Perhaps, too, it was the end of a dream.

Cliffs above the harbor named for Richard Henry Dana were of sandstone, eroded by wind and rain.
Courtesy of the San Juan Capistrano Historical Society

Chapter 2

<u>Secularization and Pueblo Beginnings</u>
<u>1821 – 1848</u>

In 1821, the year of Mexican independence from Spain, Mission San Juan Capistrano had already begun its decline. Walls that had stood forty years began to show signs of deterioration, crop and livestock production was reduced, and the number of neophytes began to fall. Instead of helping the faltering missions, the new Mexican government launched a program of secularization designed to free the Indians from mission control. The program would also free land for settlement.

The plight of the missions in California was not the concern of the neighboring United States of America. In 1821, the United States was caught up in a struggle toward economic self-sufficiency, a build-up of its military establishment, and an intensification of its westward migration. All these acts were part of a growing nationalism that manifested itself in a desire for land and the subsequent encouragement and protection of settlers. On the West Coast these same themes existed, but the migration was northward, not westward, and the nationalism was Mexican, not American.

One of the first Mexican policies to affect California was the encouragement of trade with foreign countries. According to Leo J. Friis in *Orange County Through Four Centuries*, one of the first major companies to trade with Mission San Juan Capistrano was McCullough, Hartnell and Company, who bought hides and tallow. The firm of Bryant, Sturgis and Company took over major trade in 1828.

"San Juan is the only romantic spot on the coast. The country here for several miles is high table land, running boldly to the shore, and

breaking off in a steep cliff, at the foot of which the waters of the Pacific are constantly dashing." These are the words of a Bryant-Sturgis employee, Richard Henry Dana, who described the area in his classic *Two Years Before the Mast*. Dana was a Harvard undergraduate who left school because of ill health. He exchanged his frock coat for the loose ducks of a seaman and became the first to realistically depict the roughly treated, poorly paid sailor. His book not only launched a movement to improve the life of the seaman, but gave a picturesque description of life in California in the 1830s.

One of the cliffs Dana viewed in May of 1835 is named for him — Dana Point. It was here that, according to tradition, the young sailor clambered up the incline, retrieving hides that had been thrown off the cliff to the beach below.

"Down this height we pitched the hides, throwing them as far out into the air as we could, and as they were all large, stiff, and doubled, like the cover of a book, the wind took them and they swayed and eddied about, plunging and rising in the air, like a kite when it has broken its string. As it was now low tide, there was no danger of their falling into the water; and as fast as they came to the ground, the men below picked them up, and, taking them on their heads, walked off with them to the boat."

Although the cliffs behind and to the north of the harbor are today labeled Dana Point, some oldtimers believe that the cliffs referred to by Dana were those known as "Charlie's Point," which were somewhat lower and are no longer there. The southern entrance to Dana Point

Richard Henry Dana sailed aboard a trading ship as a young man. He later wrote Two Years Before the Mast. Courtesy of Doris Walker

Harbor is approximately where these cliffs, which provided a clearer view of the mission from the sea, once stood. Other historians have placed these cliffs on the south side of San Juan Creek, the location of the adobe traditionally called the "hides storage house." The cliff marked as Dana Point today was pinpointed by George Gladden, a writer for the *Los Angeles Times*, who made his deduction in 1916 on the basis of a map drawn by a cousin of Dana's.

Throwing hides from cliffs was the most convenient way to get them to the beach. Once there, it took several trips to load them onto the ship. In the log of the Courier, which anchored off Dana Point on October 4, 1827, it stated that the entire transaction took five days. In this time negotiations were made, a list of goods needed by the mission drawn and loaded into boats in exchange for fourteen hundred hides, some tallow, and a few horns. Often if there was not enough weight in the hold of the

ship, adobe bricks and tiles were used. It is said that this rubble became part of the cobblestoned streets of Boston, the place where many of the ships originated.

Increased trade was not the only change to come to San Juan. The greatest change was in the attitude of the Mexican government toward the Franciscans. While the Spanish government had supported the work of the missionaries, the Mexican government took a less benevolent view. Father Engelhardt called José M. Echeandia, the first native Mexican to become governor of California in 1825, "an avowed enemy of the religious orders."

One of the earliest manifestations of this change in attitude was a difference in the relationship between soldiers and priests.

Catholicism was the major religion of Mexico, just as it had been in Spain. By late 1824, it would be the only religion permitted in the country. Priests were therefore venerated and respected by most of Mexico's citizens. Yet the relationship between missionary and soldier had always been tense. Records show that the Franciscans were constantly plagued by the immoral conduct of the mission guards. Though it is doubtful if they had the right to punish offenders, they undoubtedly reported them to military authorities and scolded them publicly. Yet the incident of January 23, 1832, shocked contemporaries and perhaps would not have occurred had the changes in attitude toward the missionaries not taken place. It was an attack on a priest, and it occurred in San Juan Capistrano.

The attack, according to Engelhardt, consisted of three men who brandished weapons to prevent Father Josef Barona from leaving the mission on an errand. When Father Barona refused to get off his horse, one soldier pushed it violently sideways, causing the horse to slip and fall, pinning Father Barona under it. The priest was unhurt, and the three participants — José Cañedo, Hilario Garcia, and José Alipas — were imprisoned as well as excommunicated. The incident, which took place in front of mission Indians, was a public scandal. Garcia and Alipas repented and were forgiven and released. According to Bancroft, Cañedo refused to repent and spent two years in shackles until the supreme tribunal in Mexico decreed him innocent on the basis that he had been carrying out orders. Cañedo eventually

Pryor Adobe was once a hides storage house for the mission.
It is still standing today north of the Villa San Juan Mobile Home Park on Camino Capistrano.
Courtesy of the San Juan Capistrano Historical Society

came back to Capistrano as a settler.

Trouble for the missionaries had just begun. When Echeandia became governor, he made it known he was developing a plan for emancipation of all Indians. He sent Lt. Romualdo Pacheco to San Juan Capistrano to explain the idea to remaining Juaneños. Juan Avila described Pacheco as a "tall, thin man of very good physique, extremely handsome and of elegant bearing. In his manners he was very refined and gentlemanly, as also in his moral conduct." The news he brought to the Indians was heady. A short time after his departure, San Juan firebrands staged a minor revolt demanding the arrest of Father Barona.

According to Engelhardt, Corporal Hilario Machado carried out the demand only because he was frightened of the Indians in their new role. When

the Indians were calmer, he released the padre.

In July of 1826, Governor Echeandia carried out his plan and issued a Proclamation of Emancipation, declaring that Indians when qualified should be granted Mexican citizenship and be free of mission control. The news of emancipation created mixed feelings among members of the Indian community. Some welcomed it, seeing it as a chance to get out of a system of virtual serfdom.

Leonard Pitt in *Decline of the Califomios* wrote, "The neophytes were torn tragically between a secure, authoritarian existence and a free but anarchic one. Those who had spent their lives in the shadow of the cross often rejected the proffered liberty, not out of fear of the padres' wrath, but of the uncertainties of the outer world."

Brigantines like the one here were often seen offshore as they traded with missions.
Courtesy of Doris Walker

For the next ten years the mission fell into a decline. Many Indians whom the padres had released left the area. Those who remained couldn't keep up with the work. Mustard plant spread over fields that once were carefully tended. The land was a demanding mistress; it would allow no rivals.

Alfred Robinson, a visitor to San Juan in 1829, described the mission's deterioration: "This establishment was founded in the year 1776 and though in its early years the largest in the country, yet it is now in a dilapidated state and the Indians are much neglected." He had kinder things to say about the town: "In many of the villages the residences consist of straw huts of an oval form, which, when decayed, the Indians set on fire and erect new ones. Here, however, they are built of

unburnt brick, tiled and whitewashed, forming five or six blocks or streets which present a neat, comfortable appearance."

The 1830s sealed the doom of the mission system in California. After 1831, the program of mission secularization (removing them from Franciscan control) was accelerated. Governor José Figueroa in 1833 completed the emancipation of the Indians, declaring them free and equal Mexican citizens, whether or not padres thought them ready. Captain Pablo de Portilla was sent to San Juan Capistrano to organize the Indian emancipation program which included distribution of land to Indian settlers. According to Engelhardt, Portilla attempted to organize the Indian pueblo at the San Mateo rancho, but Indians asked that they be allowed instead to keep plots of land they already cultivated near the mission. The administrator agreed and a pueblo was organized late in the year. An Indian pueblo was also formed at Las Flores, an estancia (station) of Mission San Luis Key. Adobe remains of this village are still visible on a small knoll south of Las Pulgas Road on Camp Pendleton.

Why did secularization of the missions take place? The new Mexican Constitution of 1824 called for both secularization and emancipation. Although emancipation of the Indians began two years later, it was heavily controlled and the number of Indians released from the missions was small. Rapid strides were not made until the Secularization Act of 1833 which was designed to help the Indians become self-sustaining. This act was the one that called for the formation of Indian pueblos.

California historians agree that the secularization program was part of a new liberalism which emerged among native-born Californios. The new liberalism, while not entirely anti-clerical, did seek to weaken the power of the Catholic Church in temporal matters and to cut off California's final tie to Spain. It also released thousands of acres of land to the government which would eventually be turned over to private individuals through the land-grant system.

In August of 1834, the property of ten missions, including San Juan Capistrano, was ordered confiscated by the government. Half the land was to be given to Indians and the other half "administered for the public good and support of the church." An inventory of the mission property took place, valuing the land and buildings and their contents at the $56,456. A census was also taken which listed 861 neophytes attached to the mission, some of whom were totally dependent and were cared for by the padres. Although this system appeared to be fair in theory, its practice turned into a disaster. Many Indians left the pueblo, moving to other areas where they encountered a life of poverty. Some went back to Indian villages which were formerly rancherias of the mission; others moved to "uncivilized" areas beyond the Sierra Mountains. According to Bancroft, by 1850 there were only five hundred Indians left in the entire territory which had once been the domain of Mission San Juan Capistrano with only one hundred in the pueblo. "Even by the 1850s," commented historian Leonard Pitt, "the neophytes remained a demoralized class, alternately a prey to disease, liquor, violence, submission, and exploitation."

While secularization was takings place, California was in political turmoil. A succession of

Weeds grew in the mission quadrangle where Indians were once taught trades. Decline of the mission dates back to 1821.
Courtesy of the San Juan Capistrano Historical Society

The neglected mission after 1821, drew four-footed visitors.
Mexico withdrew its support of the mission because missions were "Spanish."
Courtesy of the San Juan Capistrano Historical Society

governors had come and gone, petty squabbles occupied too much time, and regionalism (north against south) was strong. During the mid-1830s Juan Bautista Alvarado declared himself governor of California, an act which displeased the authorities in Mexico, who promptly appointed Carlos Antonio Carrillo in June of 1837. Alvarado decided not to give up without a fight.

One of their battles took place near San Juan Capistrano. Carrillo's forces marched north from San Diego, while Alvarado's marched south from Los Angeles. Carrillo's men reached the mission first, asking for news of Alvarado and intending to spend the night there. For some reason they changed their

The ruins of Mission San Juan Capistrano are evident after the earthquake of 1812.
Even after its decline, the mission was still the focal point of the community.
Courtesy of the First American Title Insurance Company

mind and slept in a nearby arroyo. According to Engelhardt, it was midnight when Ignacio Exquer, temporary superintendent of the mission, was awakened by the sudden arrival of Alvarado's men. Salvador Vallejo, one of Alvarado's supporters, was supposed to occupy the mission by conciliatory means. He did this by "sending a threat to hang all who did not instantly surrender" or as one said, he (Vallejo) "charged bayonets and rushed madly through all the mission buildings from which the foe had retired." Satisfied no one was there, the "army" settled down to some serious drinking and when they learned of the nearness of the sleeping "enemy," they quickly fired a cannon in the direction of the ocean and scared them away.

The main conflict came at Las Flores, fifteen miles south of San Juan, where Carrillo's forces had set up camp with three cannons. Alvarado and his supporter, José Castro, made their headquarters Mission San Juan Capistrano, but decided to take the initiative and attacked Carrillo's camp on April 21, 1838. According to Bancroft, the battle was "for the most part one of tongue and pen, though a cannon was once or twice fired from the corral, doing no harm." Several discussions followed and on April 23, a treaty was signed, making Alvarado the victor.

The mission did little else during these years of deterioration and neglect. The courtyard stood empty; vineyards turned brown in the sun. Resident Indians, most of them old and infirm, kept to their rooms, their only outings an occasional visit to the chapel. Only Father José Maria de Zalvidea remained to look after the spiritual needs of the community. The administration of the mission was left in the hands of an appointed superintendent. Ensign Juan José Rocha, José Antonio Pico, and Francisco Sepulveda held this post successively until the appointment of Santiago Arguello in January of 1838.

Arguello, who as a young officer had defended the village against the Bouchard invaders, was remembered by some of the older residents of the pueblo. Despite his less than courageous stand against Bouchard, Arguello had risen in the military ranks and had made quite a name for himself in San Diego. He accepted the post in San Juan for which he would be paid $1,000 per year. The money came from Indians remaining in the pueblo, who were expected to raise funds to support all government officials who were assigned to the town for reasons of the "public good." An early form of taxation, the system was exceedingly harsh because it completely ignored individual needs of Indians who often had nothing left for their own families. The case of Arguello brought the matter to a head. Arguello had several problems — a wife, twenty-two children, and numerous in-laws were the cause of most of them — and the townsfolk complained about him to authorities. On April 8, 1839, José Delfin, an Indian resident of the pueblo of San Juan Capistrano, filed a complaint.

According to Engelhardt, the complaint claimed that "the administrator cultivated fields for himself with Indian labor; that he put his brand on the best horses; that he bought animals with mission brandy. Thereupon 60 Indians who remained at work demanded an administrator who was just and who had not so large a family." An investigation ensued and Arguello was cleared. The Indians remained dissatisfied but could do nothing else but pack their meager belongings and leave, or stay and try, to live with the situation. Many chose the former solution and the mission grew poorer.

By 1840, it was apparent that the Indian pueblo had failed. Some historians believe that the cause was premature emancipation. Indians, they said, were not ready for the freedom they were given and used the opportunity to refrain from work and to indulge the vices formerly punished by the mission padres. Other historians argue that the major failure was that the promised freedom was not liberty, but a new form of servitude. Though free of Franciscan control, the Indians were still forced to care for mission property and dependents and now had the added job of supporting government administrators. They had merely exchanged masters. For that reason pueblo life was unattractive and the Indians left.

In hopes of finding a solution to the problems that beset the community, governing officials sent William Hartnell, an American, to San Juan Capistrano to investigate the situation. He also was to make arrangements for the upkeep of mission property and the support of the friar and other elderly persons who still lived and depended on the mission. During the years of secular administration, the mission had accumulated many debts and had been victimized by robbers. There was the added problem of Indian dissatisfaction with the new system. Hartnell, who was familiar with Capistrano because of the Arguello investigation, found that the Indians wanted old Father Zalvidea appointed administrator of the mission. Engelhardt explained the request as a plea for an "honest" person to represent them. They believed the secular administrators had cheated them.

There were other solutions to consider. Andres Pico had offered to rent the mission. In exchange for occupying the buildings and land, he would provide for the poor and infirm and would pay wages to Indian laborers. But he would not actually pay rent to the Indians, whom the Franciscans had considered owners of the mission property. Another solution was one proposed by J. A. Estudillo, who would become mayordomo of the mission for six years for no salary, but would receive a third of the product of the estates. He, too, offered to care for the aged, repair the buildings, and use his own equipment for tilling the fields. The Indians were not in favor of either proposal, so Hartnell appointed Father Zalvidea to be in charge of the mission until the pueblo could be reorganized.

Father Zalvidea's term lasted only a short time. Unable to cope with the massive problems, he asked a Belgian, Augustin Janssens, to take over the mayordomo duties. His choice was confirmed by the governor and Janssens stepped in. The Belgian was apparently reluctant to become the administrator of the mission. He had been living at the Trabuco Rancho, owned by Santiago Arguello, while Arguello was away filing for a land grant. He looked upon the mission as a project that had little hope because the mission was without resources. He was promised assistance from San Luis Rey and San Fernando, and he finally consented to make an attempt.

"I named two Indian alcaldes to go to Los Angeles to bring back the Indians who had all left because there had been no means of livelihood at the mission," he said in his autobiography. He also set about making repairs, the first being the zanja (water ditch) which had not been functional for fourteen years.

Located between Arroyo de Trabuco and Arroyo de la Mission Vieja (San Juan Creek), the mission had been supplied by water through a system of zanjas and underground waterways. As early as 1809, an aqueduct with a brick masonry arch had been built across a ravine near Trabuco Creek to bring water into a flume to irrigate mission vineyards. The flume ended approximately in front of the site of the old Capistrano High School tennis courts. At one time this flume extended to a distance of nearly fourteen hundred feet.

While Janssens was busy at the mission, events were taking place which would prove his original apprehensions correct. Private citizens, whom Engelhardt contemptuously refers to as "the San Diego group," were petitioning the governor for grants of land. Not only were they interested in the vast tracts that once were the ranches of the mission, they also wanted the Indian pueblo dissolved so they could own land in the town. There also was talk of selling the mission.

"When I saw what was going on, I wrote to Governor Alvarado proposing that the mission be given to me for six years, and that at the end of that time I would leave the gardens fenced and the property restored, so that there would be no need to sell the mission," said Janssens. Father Zalvidea also took up the plea, begging the governor not to sell the land that once belonged to the mission because Indians left in the pueblo would have no place to graze their cattle. If the uncertain future of the mission was not enough to worry about, the year 1841 was also one of heavy rain, and floods caused a great deal of damage.

The pleas went unheeded. In May of 1841, Governor Alvarado's secretary declared that the mission was in a ruinous state and the Indian pueblo should be dissolved. Anyone wishing to make a claim against the mission should do so promptly. In June, the San Diego group was informed that their petition for settlement of San Juan Capistrano had been granted, but Indians were to be given equal rights.

Bancroft in his *History of California* lists the names of those having obtained one hundred to three hundred varas of land. Many of the names are still familiar in the community today.

The reorganization of the pueblo marked an important change in San Juan's history. Before 1841, San Juan Capistrano did not exist as a formal

A cattle brand of Mission San Juan Capistrano is seen here. At one time the mission herds numbered fourteen thousand. Courtesy of the San Juan Capistrano Historical Society

town. Adobes clustered around the mission were homes. Indians tended gardens or worked in open fields. Manufacturing activities — soapmaking, hatmaking, weaving — took place within the mission. The new pueblo would usher in a new era. Non-Indian settlers would bring the baggage of their own civilization from which they would extract those things they considered necessary — stores, livery stables, hotels, and cantinas. They would also bring their greed and their cunning, and for this reason, San Juan Capistrano's "charter" stated that, above all else, Indians were to be protected from "unscrupulous whites."

The charter was really a set of regulations governing the establishment of the new pueblo. It was drawn by Gov. Juan B. Alvarado on July 29, 1841. In it Alvarado decreed that San Juan was to have a regular municipal government, an alcalde (mayor), ayuntamiento (council), and juez de paz (justice of the peace). The land would be divided into house lots and garden lots with farm equipment held by the governor's commissioner and distributed as needed. The land granted would have to be occupied within a year or the land could be given to someone else.

The mission still figured prominently in the plans for the town. According to the regulations, proceeds from the vineyards and orchards would be used to support the priest, who would reside in the mission and have charge of a third of the buildings. Another third of the structures would be set aside for use of travelers and the commissioner and the last third would be used by Indians who still resided in the mission. Any rents collected would be used for repairs. Manufacturing tools were to remain in the mission, but could be used by Indian workmen who had the commissioner's permission to do so. Sheep were to be cared for by one individual who would receive a third of their produce for his labors. The rest would be used for weaving.

Juan Bandini was selected to be in charge of all this activity. Richard Henry Dana described Bandini as he saw him once at a fandango (ball): "He was dressed in white pantaloons, neatly made, a short jacket of dark silk, gaily figured, white stockings and morocco slippers upon his very small feet. His slight and graceful figure was well-adapted to dancing, and he moved about with the grace and daintiness of 'a young fawn."

During Bandini's administration, which lasted less than a year, the town's name was officially changed to San Juan de Arguello, but somehow it never caught on.

The plans for the town, like the name, faded away. Only a few ex-neophytes and the four or five white families who had lived in the area a long time occupied their land. According to Bandini, the town was demoralized because unscrupulous persons had flocked to the pueblo under the pretense of becoming settlers and vice and crime flourished. Bandini left in March of 1842, disclaiming responsibility for the seriousness of the situation. Janssens was temporarily left in charge of the town and in April, Augustin Olvera was appointed justice of the peace. He was reappointed for 1843, but Rosario Aguilar succeeded him in mid-year. He was followed by Emigdio Vejar and then John Forster, who began his term in July of 1845. The job was tough and unpopular. The local justice was required to settle disputes involving brands, possession of property, wagers, promissory notes — even guardianships. The justice also heard criminal cases, and had the authority to prescribe punishments, even death.

Most justices resigned after a short period of service. Sometimes resignations were not accepted,

Hides and tallow trade, begun in the mission period, continued after land grants divided land into ranchos.
Courtesy of the San Juan Capistrano Historical Society

Left to right: Maraneta Alvarado, Ignacia Alvarado de Pico (wife), Pio Pico, and Trinidad de la Guerra.
Courtesy of the First American Title Insurance Company

so the men continued to serve half-heartedly. Bandini called troublemakers "drones" who practiced "thieving, drunkenness and some other deeds deserving to be styled crimes." Historian Leonard Pitt provided a clue when he said it was the practice of the Mexican government to empty the jails of Sonora and Sinaloa in order to find colonists for the California frontier. Undoubtedly, some of the offenders were impoverished Indians who had learned all too well the ways of the white man in the streets of El Pueblo de Nuestra Senora de la Reina de Los Angeles.

It is difficult to judge the number of people left in the town at that time. A census taken in the Los Angeles territory in 1844 listed only Rosario Aguilar, Emigdio Vejar, his wife and children, Martino Subira, and Manuel Varelas as residents of San Juan Capistrano. Indians, of course, were frequently omitted from padrons (rolls), but in view of the number of petitioners for land in 1841, one suspects that this census might not have been completed.

One of the oldest residents to depart in 1842 was Father Zalvidea, who had served the mission since 1826. Old and sick, he left the mission for San Luis Rey, never to return. No resident priest inhabited the mission after him until 1846 and it was said that people made bonfires of documents and used the buildings of the mission for immoral purposes. Governor Manuel Micheltorena, who succeeded Alvarado, suggested that the mission be returned to the Franciscans, but it was too late. The mission system, which once had charge of fifteen thousand souls and thousands of acres of land, was already dead. Of the property of Mission San Juan Capistrano, only five yoke of oxen remained. Yet the mission still stood, its brown walls shrinking into the soil, its wooden windows staring blindly into the courtyard where scores of Indians once worked in the sun. The Indians were gone; so were the grey-robed friars. Only the wind remained, stirring the

John Forster, who bought Mission San Juan Capistrano at public auction,
once owned 200,000 acres of land.
Courtesy of the San Juan Capistrano Historical Society

Yisdora Pico Forster, wife of John Forster, was sister of the last Mexican governor.
Courtesy of the San Juan Capistrano Historical Society

*The south east wing of the mission was once used as a chapel until the Serra Chapel was restored. It is now a gift shop.
Courtesy of the San Juan Capistrano Historical Society*

weeds that choked the walkways, whispering through empty rooms, caressing the bells whose ropes remained coiled, untouched, unwanted. Yet the mission was not dead, only asleep. In seventy five years, it would awaken to the gentle touch of love.

In 1845, Mission San Juan Capistrano was nothing more than a debt-ridden burden to its declared owner, the government. In December, Pio Pico, the last of the Mexican governors of California, formally disposed of it.

"Pico, usually overhung with gold chains and jewels, his pockets filled with $50 gold pieces, sold the mission at auction to his brother-in-law, John Forster, and James McKinley for $710," wrote Mrs. Older. Forster, who was destined to become one of the largest landowners in California, had already

acquired Rancho Trabuco and Rancho Mission Vieja, which was also known as Rancho La Paz. He moved to Capistrano in 1844, and after his purchase of the mission, he and his family moved into it. He also became the owner of several original portreros of the mission (farming areas). These were Portrero Los Pinos, El Carrizo, and La Cienega. He added to his holdings, acquiring Rancho Los Desechos (part of San Clemente today) and Pico's own Rancho Santa Margarita Las Flores (Camp Pendleton). According to family records, at one time Forster owned over 250,000 acres of land. It is interesting to note that in an interview with Pico done in 1877 he (Pico) does not even mention the sale of the mission to Forster. He says only that it was sold to McKinley. This was probably because of a celebrated dispute between Pico and Forster which resulted in a lawsuit over the ownership of the Santa Margarita Ranch, which Forster won.

The mission property, taken over by Forster and his wife and children in 1845, included the buildings, grounds, and orchards. The Catholic Church was allowed to keep Father Serra's chapel and a small room for the priest to live in.

The fate of the mission was soon overshadowed by another event, one that would bring changes undreamed of by the local population. It was the coming of war.

War between Mexico and the United States was declared by Congress on May 9, 1846. By July the American flag was flying in Monterey, supplanting the Bear flag which had flown for only one month. Although no battles were waged in San Juan Capistrano (indeed only one noteworthy battle occurred in all of Southern California), two incidents took place near the mission. Both involved the mission's new owner, Don Juan Forster.

"Fremont and his whole force (Kit Carson, Alexander Godey, and the Indian company of Shawnees with him) surrounded the mission buildings at San Juan Capistrano believing that I would attempt to escape," wrote Forster. "He was savage against me until we had an explanation when he became convinced that I was favorably disposed to the U.S. at the same time that I was trying to save the interests of my relatives, the Pico family."

The date of this incident is not given but it is likely that it occurred after Commodore John Drake Sloat took over Monterey and his successor, Commodore Robert Field Stockton, sent Fremont and his California Battalion of Volunteers to "pacify" the south. Because Pico is mentioned, it must have occurred after August 10, when Pico fled Los Angeles and was hidden for a month by Forster at the Santa Margarita Rancho.

Another incident, much less dramatic, took place January 5, 1847, when Stockton and Stephen W. Kearny visited San Juan Capistrano on their way north after the battle of San Pasqual. In the diary of Maj. W. H. Emory, the mission's Great Stone Church ruins were described along with a notation that a house had been seen with a brush fence around the door. Inside were four Californios dying from wounds received in the battle of San Pasqual. Emory commented that the group proceeded to the Alisos Rancheria where "through the kindness of Mr. Forster, an Englishman, we received here a supply of fresh horses." Apparently Forster's loyalties were no longer questioned.

The Treaty of Guadalupe-Hidalgo, marking the end of the Mexican War and the cession of California to the United States, was ratified by the Congress on March 10, 1848. A new era was about to begin in San Juan Capistrano.

This is typical clothing styles of the rancho owners and their vaquaros. Courtesy of the San Juan Capistrano Historical Society

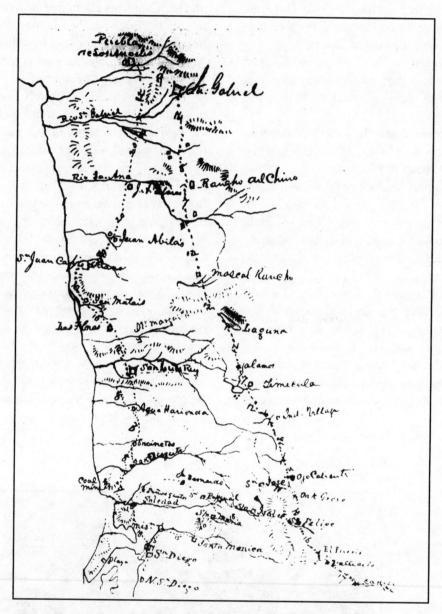

Here is El Camino Real drawn in 1850 by Lt. Cave J. Coutts. The "King's highway" linked the missions.
Courtesy of the San Juan Capistrano Historical Society

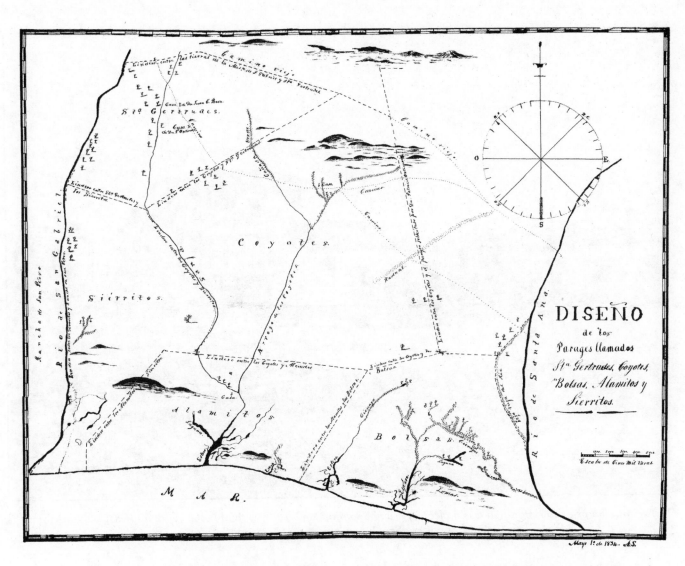

*A land grant map shows Rancho Los Coyotes in northern Orange County. Each Mexican grant
had its own official diseno, or sketch, showing its boundaries.
Courtesy of the Long Beach Historical Society*

The mission prior to restoration was a place of crumbling roofs and walls, with only the south and east sections intact.
Courtesy of the San Juan Capistrano Historical Society

Chapter 3

Ranchos, Bandits, and Yanks
1848 – 1887

Gold was hidden in the bowels and the foothills of the California Sierra, overlooked by the Spaniards ignored by the Indians. If gold had appeared in Indian villages, Spaniards would have to find its source. But Indians weren't interested in gold so it remained hidden until 1848 when its discovery in the Sacramento Valley launched a movement which transformed California overnight. News of the find spread quickly to the East Coast, temporarily replacing slavery, industrialization, and westward settlement as the major topics in taverns, inns, general stores, and drawing rooms. Gold fever brought people, statehood, and rapid social change. Thousands sold everything and went to California, little knowing they would be the instruments of a cultural transplant that would conquer California more thoroughly than any military action had.

Northern California erupted into a frenzy of boisterous activity, but Southern California remained temporarily calm and aloof, only obliquely touched by the events taking place in the North. In Southern California the most sweeping change had taken place a decade earlier. The decline of the authority of the missions had elevated the rancheros (grantees of land) into the leaders of the new social order. Rancheros now held the land, cattle, and the benefits of foreign trade. They also held the Indians, many of whom had turned to the rancheros for a means of livelihood.

In the midst of sprawling, cattle-covered ranches was San Juan Capistrano, a small frontier town plagued by squatters, drifters, and bandits. Men swaggered through town with pistols on their hips; drunken vaqueros (cowboys) brawled in the streets on Saturday nights. The apparent chaos which followed the founding of the pueblo had not entirely disappeared. Yet the promise of permanence was already present. Neat rows of corn pushed through the soil behind each adobe; fine new townhouses lined the plaza, monuments to the landowners who transacted business with merchants from the sea. And the mission still stood, a symbol of the past, defying the wind, rain, and indifference which threatened its future.

The mission was now the home of Don Juan Forster, one of the wealthiest landowners in Southern California. His family occupied the rooms that are today the museum and gift shop. The rest of the mission was left to the elements. Horace Bell in his *Reminiscences of a Ranger or Early Times in Southern California* described a brief visit to the former mission during a bandit hunt in the 1850s. "We reached San Juan Capistrano late at night and roused Juan Forster who inhabited the only inhabitable part of the old, dilapidated, vermin-infested, tumbling down mission buildings." Forster allowed the rangers to camp there for the night, an experience which Bell said was decidedly unpleasant. One other person inhabited the mission, Father Jose Maria Rosales, the town's first secular priest. Franciscans had returned to the mission church in 1846, but when Father Rosales stopped there on his way to Mexico in 1850, he found the place temporarily without a spiritual counselor. Concerned, he decided to postpone his journey and remained until 1853.

San Juan Capistrano at mid-century was a town in the throes of growth. On the El Camino Real half way between Los Angeles and San Diego, San Juan was a convenient stopping place for prospectors on

A view of the mission from the French Hotel shows the original town plaza.
Courtesy of the San Juan Capistrano Historical Society

their way to the gold fields, travelers going south, and vaqueros who wandered wherever work was to be found. The town was built around a central plaza, or village square, bounded on the north by the mission, on the east by the main road called Calle Oriental (East Street), on the west by Calle Central (Center Street), and on the south a short street called Cross Street which probably didn't have a name. Today we call Calle Oriental by its original name, El Camino Real; Calle Central is called Camino Capistrano, and Cross Street is named Yorba Street. Adobe buildings, attached to one another by common walls, lined the east and west sides of the plaza. Some of these buildings were homes, while others were stores, cantinas, or home-shop combinations. In 1857, the east side of the plaza contained the homes of Jose M. Canedo, Blas Aguilar, and Jose Parra, and the stores of Henry Charles, Michael Kraszewski, and the shop-home of shoemaker Tomas Burruel. The west side contained the homes of the Valenzuelas, the block-long hacienda of Juan Avila, the home and store of Manuel Garcia, possibly the store of George Pflugardt, the homes of Domingo and Miguel Yorba, and the building which served as the jail, justice court, and stage stop. South of the Burruel Adobe in an area which today would include the Sizzler and the shopping center developed by the Stroscher family was a walled area known as the mission orchards. Mission gardens also occupied what today we would call the area between Spring Street and

Ortega Highway and failed the area directly west of the mission as far as Los Rios Street. Because Los Rios ran along the west side of the mission it was called Calle Occidental (West Street). Calle Central met a dead end at the mission entrance and ranch of course Calle Oriental ran along the east side of the mission and on towards Los Angeles. Adobes dotted Los Rios Street, and the banks of both the Trabuco and San Juan Creek.

Indians who owned land had trouble keeping it. Judge Benjamin Hayes, a frequent visitor to San Juan Capistrano, wrote in his Pioneer Notes in 1856 that Indians had come to him complaining that Sonorans had usurped their land in Capistrano. The outcome of these complaints is not noted. Hayes, who served as district judge from 1853 to 1864, traveled throughout the region to hold court. Because of the lawlessness of the period, he carried a bowie knife and a double-barrelled shotgun at all times and his diaries are filled with colorful accounts of his escapades. Hayes was frequently called upon to settle cases involving land disputes, many of them accusing Sonorans of squatting.

Thousands of Sonorans had entered California during the gold rush and because many were successful they earned the enmity of jealous Yankees. Historians point out there was a great deal of discrimination against Mexicans in the gold country. Because of mistreatment, many were forced to return home or settle in other parts of the state. Some apparently chose San Juan Capistrano and squatted on land they thought they might be able to keep.

Because Yankees frequently failed to distinguish between foreigners and native-born Californios, many of the latter also felt the sting of discrimination and were discouraged from prospecting in the gold fields.

Those fortunate enough to own ranches didn't have to look for gold. The hides and tallow trade established by the missions was still lucrative and new markets for beef had opened in the northern mining camps. Rancheros made more than enough money to support a way of life based on large families, polished manners, material comforts, and the pleasure of living. But life based on an almost feudalistic pattern clashed with the culture brought in by the Yankees. In the words of historian Leonard Pitt, "This clash involved elements such as the Protestant's condescension toward Catholicism; the Puritan's dedication to work, now familiarly known as the 'Protestant ethic'; the republican's loathing of aristocracy; the Yankees' belief in manifest destiny; and the Anglo-Saxon's generalized fear of racial mixture." Pitt conceded that some adjusted to life in California and accepted it on its own terms. But these, he said, were mostly members of the trading or seafaring class who had dealt with rancheros on a different level than farmers, trappers, and drifters in and out of the gold fields.

Not everyone was a landowner, but because the rancho was like a self-contained community with its own craftsmen, cooks, cowboys, field hands, and household staff, a large number of people found employment on them. Some people worked for themselves while a few labored outside the law. Indian raids plagued the rancheros, particularly if their land extended to the outskirts of the "civilized" portions of California. But there was a worse problem. In the words of Robert Glass Cleland in *Cattle on a Thousand Hills*, outlaws caused the most trouble: "Much as they suffered from Indian depredations, the rancheros paid far heavier tolls to the cattle thieves and other outlaw bands which then infested Southern California. As early as 1851, Gov. Peter H. Burnett listed stock rustling as one of the

Canedo Adobe, now gone, was home of Salvador Canedo, who brought smallpox in 1862, when sailors infected with the disease brought lumber to repair his home.
Courtesy of Alfonso Yorba

state's major economic ills and sought to have it made a capital offense."

Residents of frontier mining camps needed little provocation for hanging foreigners, particularly Mexicans. This attitude of contempt and hatred may have spawned the roving bands of banditos that terrorized California during the rancho era. Perhaps the reasons went deeper. The Californio outlaws might have believed they were avenging the conquest of California by not only lashing out against the gringos who had forced their way into their culture, but also against the rancheros who had let the gringos in without a fight. Or the creation of the bandit class might have been the result of the concentration of wealth in the hands of a few and the lack of social and economic mobility. Perhaps it had something to do with the reassertion of masculinity by men who had been forced into peonage, whose women were coveted by gringos in a place where white women were scarce, and who needed an identity of their own.

San Juan Capistrano was not isolated from this social problem. Though Juan Avila had a reputation

Burruel Adobe, home of "Chola" Martina, now gone. Martina was the sweetheart of Juan Flores, a bandit who raided the town in 1857.
Courtesy of Alfonso Yorba

agreeably. I remember noticing that his coat was torn and remarked to him that a vaquero should always carry needle and thread with him and I gave him some."

They rode off, failing to pay for the pistol. Irritated, Kraszewski rode after them and caught up with Varelas, whom he knew, asking him why his friend hadn't paid. Varelas rode back with him to the store as though intending to take care of the matter, but then abruptly rode off again.

Two minutes later the entire gang thundered into town, pistols in hand, and surrounded the store. Townsfolk scattered. The street was quiet, tense. Everyone waited.

for dealing swiftly and harshly with cattle and horse thieves, there was nevertheless some sympathy toward the bandit class. Oral tradition of San Juan is rich in stories of bandits and their deeds, in which the outlaws regard San Juan as a refuge, a place where their families, friends, and sweethearts live. One story exemplifies these tales, a story retold so often that, although true, can today rival the tallest tales of the most talented storytellers. It took place in January of 1857 and is known as the Juan Flores Uprising. Several versions of the event exist today. The fairest and most authentic version appears to be the one told by participant Michael Kraszewski. The account, prepared for Hubert Howe Bancroft, was corroborated by Juan Forster.

The incident began with an innocent visit to Kraszewski's store, located on the east side of El Camino Real at the edge of the plaza. Flores, Antonio Maria Varelas (nephew of Juan Avila), and Juan Cartabo wandered into the store, browsed for a while, then Cartabo bought a pistol, taking it outside to shoot at something in the street. They said they were on their way to San Luis Rey to become vaqueros.

"The chief — Flores — I liked his appearance quite well when he came into my store," recalled Kraszewski. "He was civil in manner and spoke

Librado Silvas, a customer in the store, bolted the front door and he and Kraszewski held the side door with their hands. A shot rang out, splitting the wood of the door, grazing Silvas' wrist. He spun away in pain and tried to hide.

A voice outside, that of neighbor Pedro Verdugo, shouted at Varelas, telling him to go away and to leave Kraszewski alone. Varelas answered by breaking down Kraszewski's door.

"I sat down behind the counter with a big Spanish basket covering me," said Kraszewski. "I looked upon myself as lost."

Not finding (or ignoring) the Pole, they plundered the store, taking what they wanted and hauling the rest into the street. Then they left.

Everyone thought they'd gone for good. Those who were reluctant to say anything before, talked freely. Kraszewski learned that Flores and some of the others had just escaped from San Quentin where they had been sent for horse-stealing. Some of the members of the gang were known to some of the local residents and had tried to hide their identities.

Most of the gang members were quite young. Varelas, whose nickname was Chino, was only a teenager. Flores, who was considered co-leader of the gang along with Pancho Daniel, was only twenty-two. The size of the gang in San Juan was eleven. Other sources claim it was between fifty and one hundred, including men who joined for quasi-political reasons, men seeking vengeance, and those who had escaped with Flores. The extended group called itself the Manilas (shackles) and was blamed for several incidents of theft and other crimes in the Los Angeles area.

They came back to San Juan Capistrano entering quietly this time, going first to the home of shoemaker Tomas Burruel. Burruel's housekeeper was a young girl nicknamed Chola Martina who was supposedly Flores' sweetheart. They waited for dusk.

Kraszewski was dining that night at the home of his friend Juan Forster when a messenger rushed in with the news that George Pflugardt had been shot and the whole town was in an uproar. Forster decided to go out and try to calm people down, but his friends persuaded him to stay out of it because the bandits were stationed all over town.

"He heeded our wishes and most particularly the supplications of his own wife and several other families that had rushed into his house for protection," said Kraszewski.

Forster's brother, Thomas, and his friend Miguel Verdugo ventured out to see what was going on. A shot rang out and they retreated back into the house (the former mission). They joined the others who were watching the proceedings from a safe vantage point. Because the mission faced the town plaza they had a good view of what was taking place. The bandits, interspersed through town, were not letting anyone in or out.

The silence of the night was broken by the sound of a single rider coming into town. It was Jose Parra who lived next to Henry Charles' store. The bandits let him pass. The street was littered with debris, remnants of the plunder of the stores of Henry Charles, George Pflugardt, and Michael Kraszewski. At this point they had not touched the

"Chola" Martina Burruel, thought to be a witch, was once a sweetheart of a bandit.
Courtesy of San Juan Capistrano Historical Society

store of Manuel Garcia. It was well-organized for defense.

At 2:00 a.m., they prepared to leave.

Among those hiding in the mission were two Americans. One was Garnet Hardy. Two years earlier a team of Hardy's horses had been stolen by Flores. It was that crime that had sent him to prison. Now the bandit was here and in an ugly frame of mind. Forster decided that Hardy and the other American should leave. He instructed Brigido Morillo, an oldtimer, to take the two Americans to Los Angeles over the mountains by way of El Lago

Machado (Elsinore). It would be safer.

One account says that Hardy personally spread the word of the Flores attack. Another says that a boy on horseback brought the news to the sheriff in Los Angeles. Still another says that Hardy wrote the news to his brother, having recognized the bandits earlier.

However informed, Sheriff James Barton immediately organized a posse which set off on Thursday night.

The posse arrived early in the morning at the ranch of Jose Sepulveda. There they were warned that the bandits were armed and dangerous and numbered about fifty. According to a report in the *Los Angeles Star*, the information was shrugged off and the men proceeded. Twelve miles from Sepulveda's ranch (fifteen miles north of San Juan Capistrano) the posse saw a lone rider approaching. Riding forward to meet him, the men found themselves suddenly surrounded by members of the gang. Both sides drew their pistols and fired. Three bandits fell with the first round of shots; Sheriff Barton, William Little, Charles Baker, and Charles Daly also died. Frank Alexander, one of the Hardy brothers, and the guide survived and fled back to Los Angeles.

When the survivors reached town and told their story, forty men mounted and set off after the bandits. On Saturday morning another group of about fourteen joined the search, but these were after the bodies. Finding them, they noticed they had been fired upon repeatedly at close range, as though someone had tried to kill them over and over again. Then they'd been stripped of their valuables, including their boots. The grisly remains were removed from the road (about where Laguna Freeway meets the San Diego Freeway) and taken home to Los Angeles where they were paraded through the streets. Two armed posses took up the search after the burial — one posse was the Monte Company (Yankees) and the other the California Company (Californios) led by Don Andres Pico.

The bandits would be hard to catch.

Immediately after the gun battle, the bandits turned around and came back to Capistrano. Reckless now, they surrounded Forster's home and demanded that he give them Henry Charles, who had taken refuge at the Forster's, and a horse. Forster refused.

"Charles was frightened to death, crying like a child," said Kraszewski. "The ladies, by sheer force, dragged him and stowed him away under a bed and covered him up with their clothing."

Unwilling to storm Forster's home, the gang left, invaded Garcia's store, took twenty-four dollars in goods, and left.

The manhunt went on for days. Finally, with the help of forty-three Indians who volunteered to find the camp of the outlaws, the gang was found in a narrow canyon near Saddleback Mountain.

Varelas, who apparently decided it was in his best interest to turn informer, crept into the night and told one of the Indians the best place for the posse to attack the camp. But the position of the moon prevented the attack and Flores and some of his men escaped up the side of the

The family of Juan Avila poses in front of Avila Adobe in the 1870s. The adobe was destroyed by fire and portions were later rebuilt. Courtesy of the Charles W. Bowers Museum

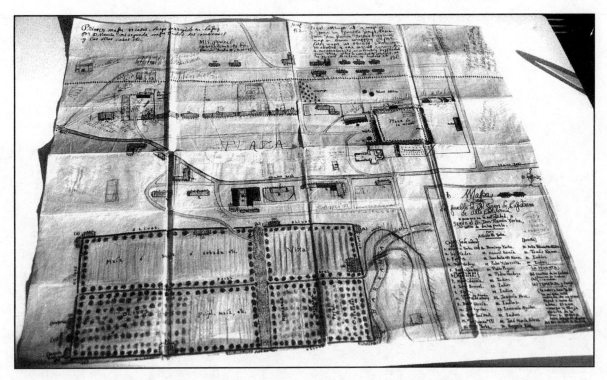

A map drawn by Ramon Yorba shows the town in 1850.
Courtesy of Mike Darnold

mountain. Varelas, meanwhile, fled to the posse.

"The mountain to which the robbers had fled (now called Flores Peak in Modjeska Canyon) was almost inaccessible, even on foot, and while the Americans were ascending the hill, Juan Flores, Jesus Espinosa, and Leonardo Lopez slid their horses down a precipice to a kind of shelf about fifty feet below where they abandoned them and escaped down a precipitous ledge of rocks, about five hundred feet high, by aid of the brush growing on its side," noted the *Los Angeles Star*. Then they made their way to the next hill and proceeded through the dense chaparral on foot.

Francisco Ardillero and Juan "Cartabo were caught. Half of the American company followed Flores' trail until they found him and his two companions and overpowered them. The three were taken to the ranch of Teodocio Yorba. Somehow, during the night, they escaped. According to the Star, when Andres Pico heard about Flores' escape, he immediately hanged Cartabo and Ardillero.

Flores was recaptured alone in the Simi Pass, north of Los Angeles. He was jailed and awaited execution. Other members of his gang (some of them were only alleged members) were not given formal legal treatment, according to an account in the Star published February 14, 1857:

"The people having taken the administration of justice into their own hands, the death penalty has been inflicted on the following persons: Juan Cartabo alias Juan Sanripa, alias Juan Silvas; Francisco alias Guerro Ardillero; Jose Santos, Diego Navarro, Pedro Lopez, Juan Valenzuela, Jesus Espinosa, and Encarnacion Berryessa. Three other names were unknown."

It was later discovered that three of those hanged had not actually allied themselves with the gang. The mistake was regretted, but nothing must stand in the way of justice.

Flores, a model prisoner, politely answered the questions of all who came to see him. One of these was Kraszewski who asked him what had occurred the day of the murder in San Juan. Flores answered that Chola Martina had a rebozo (shawl) in pawn at Pflugardt's for ten dollars. At Flores' urging, she went to the store at dusk to ask to take her rebozo out. Pflugardt had two rooms, one was a bar in charge of a Mexican named Femando Perez and the other was the store which contained an arsenal which the gang needed. Pflugardt wanted to bring the rebozo

The cattle industry gained new prominence after gold was discovered in 1848 in Northern California.
Courtesy of the San Juan Capistrano Historical Society

into the bar but Chola Martina said no.

"As the store had no windows, only one door in front and another on the side street, he opened the front door to get light. The woman laid $10 in silver on the counter and he turned around to look for the rebozo (on the shelf behind). She then lighted a cigarrito, went to the door and smoked so the light could be seen outside. The bandits were under a pear tree 50 to 100 yards distant," wrote Kraszewski, recounting what Flores told him. Three bandits then went into the store, one firing from behind Chola and the others firing at the same time from other positions. He fell down, uttered the words "my child" and died.

One account claims that Flores and his gang then ordered the employee in the next room to fix them dinner and they sat and ate it while Pflugardt's blood drained out of his body. Another account says that the bandits took Pflugardt to the town square and hanged him. Another story says that Chola Martina was able to get the shopkeeper to open his door because he desired her. Yet another credits her with riding to Sepulveda's ranch and tampering with the sheriffs and his posse's guns while they ate breakfast inside so that the guns wouldn't fire. If the survivors are to be believed, there was nothing wrong with the guns, there were just too many bandits.

Although the bandits were caught and either imprisoned or hanged, Chola Martina seems to have been ignored by the lawmen. She continued to live in San Juan until 1910 in the Burruel Adobe.

Juan Flores was hanged at a public execution

in Los Angeles on Valentine's Day, 1857, without a formal trial. After the decision was made by the vigilantes, the mob marched to the jail and took possession of Flores.

"The prisoner walked with firmness and seemed as composed as anyone in the crowd," wrote a reporter for the Star. "The distance from the jail to the hill on which the scaffold was erected, is about a quarter of a mile. The prisoner was dressed in white pants, light vest and black merino sack coat. He was a young man, about 22 years of age, and of pleasing countenance. There was nothing in his appearance to indicate the formidable bandit which he had proved himself to be."

He was led to his place of execution, accompanied by two priests. His arms were tied to his body and he ascended the steps. He asked to speak. The crowd fell silent. He said he was ready to die, that he had committed many crimes. He had no ill will against any man. He hoped no one would bear ill will against him. He repeated he was ready to die. He gave instructions for his burial to some people standing nearby whom he recognized and then asked that his face be covered with a white handkerchief. It was. The plank under him dropped away. His body swung from the noose. The fall was too short. The victim swung in agony for a considerable time. In his struggle, his arm ropes loosened and he attempted to get the rope from his neck. His executioners rushed to release his hold. Finally the limbs were still. The body hung for an hour and was taken down. The crowd dispersed. Justice had been done.

In time other members of the gang were captured and most of them hanged. Pancho Daniel won a change of venue so the mob took him out of jail and strung him up. Varelas, who had important relatives, was released.

Garcia Adobe in 1878 became the French Hotel. Today it is the only two story Monterey style adobe left in Orange County. It still stands on Camino Capistrano.
Courtesy of the San Juan Capistrano Historical Society

Sheep are seen here in front of Juzgado and Miguel Yorba Adobes en route to a river crossing.
The buildings are today the El Adobe Restaurant.
Courtesy of the San Juan Capistrano Historical Society

San Juan recovered from the incident, but from then on gained a reputation as a place of violence. Orange County historian Jim Sleeper said from the time of the Flores incident to the late 1920s, Capistrano had "one good murder a year."

The coming of the Yanks had brought many changes. Not only did the status of the Californios change, so did the status of their land. The Treaty of Guadalupe Hidalgo had guaranteed property rights, yet the Land Act of 1851 seemed to strip them away. Those who claimed to own land now had to prove it before the U.S. Land Commission within two years or forfeit it. This was a costly, time-consuming process which required a trip to San Francisco where the tribunal sat, and extensive attorney's fees. Often transfers of property were verbal and if written documents had existed, but were misplaced, witnesses had to be located who had been present during the property survey or the act of juridical possession. The process forced every

landowner to spend huge sums of money and created both social and economic chaos.

One of the early claimants was Bishop Joseph Sadoc Alemany, who contested the right of the Mexican governors to sell the missions and asked that they be restored to the ownership of the Catholic Church. After lengthy consideration, the commission decided that the sale of the missions had been illegal. In 1865, the five tracts of Mission San Juan Capistrano were officially restored to the Catholic Church. The document, authorizing the return, was signed by President Abraham Lincoln.

Included in the tracts returned to the church were two marked new cemetery. They were located below Mission Hill, along El Homo Street, yet the actual new cemetery is located east of the mission, about three-quarters of a mile away, on a knoll above Los Cerritos Street. The earliest grave is that of a Forster child, marked 1847. Yet according to Father Engelhardt, the old cemetery on the mission grounds was used until the early 1860s, when a smallpox epidemic made it too dangerous to bury dead close to town. It is not known if any burials took place below Mission Hill, but when the mission land was returned to the church, burials continued to take place near the Forster crypt. The cemetery above Los Cerritos Street became the official mission cemetery (being formally deeded by James Sheehan in the early 1870s) and Mission Flats eventually became a residential district.

In 1864, having lost their title the Forsters moved out of the mission and onto their ranch at Santa Margarita y Las Flores which Pio Pico had deeded to them the same year. Pico later tried to regain the ranch in a celebrated lawsuit, but failed. The Picos' right to the land (which was, by then, the Forsters' right to it) was upheld by the U.S. Land Commission in a patent signed by President Rutherford B. Hayes in 1879.

Curiously enough, the boundaries of San Juan Capistrano township and ownership of land within those boundaries was never determined and this left many property owners with unconfirmed deeds. The failure to establish permanent rights to land with the U.S. government would cause problems for some owners in later years. But in 1850, most parcels were uncontested and having personal plats surveyed probably seemed unnecessary.

The years that followed were lean ones for San Juan. Visitors continued to pass through, many riding the stagecoach to and from Los Angeles and San Diego, two busy, growing towns. The first stage line had been put on the El Camino Real in 1852 by Phineas Banning and D. W. Alexander. Others followed, the most famous being the Seely and Wright Express, which boasted it could make the trip in twenty-four hours. Travel by stage was convenient but not without its problems. The coaches were often uncomfortable; the journey was long, and highwaymen were still troublesome. Juan Flores was gone, but others had taken his place. In 1862, the gang of Manuel Marquez plundered the territory between San Juan and Santa Ana. His gang had a rival, a group of men who hid their faces behind masks while they stole cattle, horses, and the valuables of travelers.

Outlaws were not the major worry of the 1860s. The decade began badly; it would grow worse. Harsh changes would take place that would rot the fabric of the existing social pattern beyond repair. It began, innocently, with rain.

Rain was usually welcome in the semi-acid climate of San Juan Capistrano. But in 1861, when the first shots of the Civil War were fired on the East Coast, the skies of Southern California poured out their sorrow in sheets of rain that tore into adobe walls and carried away soil, chickens, loose belongings, and all hopes of a good crop for the coming year. Caught between two raging rivers, San Juan was covered by floods and when the waters receded, people prayed and gave thanks, little knowing that the worst was yet to come.

The rain stopped, but in a year's time many wished for its return. A series of droughts struck Southern California, one after another, scorching the land until the grass shriveled into dust. Swift rivers of a year before dried to a trickle; cattle moved slowly, their huge bodies parched beyond endurance. The air was heavy with the smell of death.

Death came. Silently, indiscriminately the

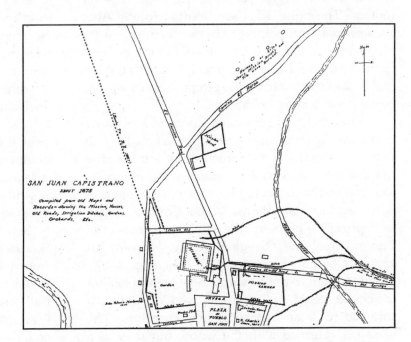

Lands restored to the Catholic Church by the U.S. Land Commission in 1860 included the main grounds and four off site tracts of the mission, including one not shown which was a garden. Courtesy of the San Juan Capistrano Historical Society

The old Mission Cemetery was acquired in the 1870s from James Sheehan.
Some burials may have taken place earlier.
Courtesy of the San Juan Capistrano Historical Society

The disease took its toll and moved on. The drought remained, reaching its height in 1864. Out of eight thousand cattle, Juan Avila had eight hundred left. While giving testimony in his famous trial over ownership of the Santa Margarita Ranch, Don Juan Forster recalled that the entire area was almost "depopulated of cattle." He added that nothing like that had ever before happened in California.

Drought and disease which decimated entire herds and destroyed almost an entire Indian labor force set the stage for the end of the ranches. But one other factor played a major role in this drama of decline — the state property tax. From the beginning of statehood the legislature was dominated by northern mining interests and laws passed by them tended to place the burden of taxation on the south. According to historian Robert Glass Cleland, the purpose of these laws was to break up the large land-holdings of the cattle dons so that land could be opened for agriculture. Governor Peter H. Burnett in 1851 believed that enforced subdivision of large tracts of land by means of direct taxation was a worthwhile endeavor. Individual rights had to bow to the public good.

In *The Cattle on a Thousand Hills*, Cleland said the situation became so bad that in 1859 southern landowners tried to secede. Andres Pico, a legislator from Los Angeles, introduced a joint resolution in the state legislature asking that the then existing counties that made up Southern California — San Luis Obispo, Santa Barbara, Los Angeles, San Bernardino, and San Diego — be withdrawn from California and be formed into a new entity called the territory of Colorado. The division bill had strong support, was approved in the state legislative houses, and was ratified by the affected counties. But it died in the Congress of the United States.

Rancheros had no other recourse. Defense of land titles, borrowing at compound interest, and

germs of the black smallpox entered almost every home. Indians were hardest hit. The mission death register, between the dates of November 16 and December 31, 1862, recorded 129 deaths — all Indians. The same fall, Cave Coutts wrote to Abel Steams that smallpox raged in San Juan where six to eight per day were being buried. In his memoirs, Ramon Yorba recalled that trenches had to be dug and bodies thrown in on top of one another so that burial could take place quickly.

The epidemic continued into 1863 in other Southern California areas, though it seemed to ebb in San Juan. The last recorded death attributed to the disease was Salvador Canedo who, ironically, was credited with having brought it. According to San Juan historian Alfonso Yorba, Canedo wanted to improve his home on the southeast corner of El Camino Real and Ortega Highway. He sent his vaqueros to San Francisco with a herd of cattle, ordering them to return with a boat-load of lumber which he would use to install wooden floors, a shingled roof, and spacious new corridors. The vaqueros returned with the wood, but they also brought the germs of the black smallpox. The resulting epidemic killed two hundred people in the town, including Salvador.

maintaining a way of life that had become obsolete had depleted their reserves. With their cattle dead no money came in to pay for necessities, let alone to pay taxes. The most prominent names in Southern California crept onto delinquent tax rolls. Parts of ranches had to be sold, many at bargain prices, to make ends meet. The gay life of rodeos, fiestas, barbecues, and horse races came to an end.

The end came quickly for some, slowly for others. A few, like Juan Avila and Juan Forster, had enough money put aside to make a partial recovery. Others hung on as long as possible, selling their land in small parcels whenever it became necessary. But the days of the California pastorale were over, days when a dozen men could stand on as many hilltops and never see the end of their land, when business transactions among friends were sealed with a handshake, when young girls in flowing mantillas swayed to the music of guitars in candlelit haciendas. The walls of the haciendas would crack, the young girls would grow old and die, but the echoes of those days would never be silenced — today, one hundred years later, we can hear them still.

As the ranches had replaced the mission, a new social and economic order based on diversified farming now replaced the ranches. New settlers, encouraged by the end of the Civil War, the new availability of land, and flowery travel guides that touted the state as a virtual paradise, flooded California. Some took advantage of the Homestead Act; others squatted on land which was owned by Californios with unconfirmed deeds.

Most settlers were farmers. Richard Egan bought acreage near Trabuco Creek for $1.25 per acre and settled down to farming barley, which he sold to Seely and Wright for 50 cents a bushel. Joel Congdon planted English walnuts (between Alipaz and Del Obispo) thus starting the walnut industry in Orange County. The Daneris' settled on the north side of the Trabuco-San Juan Creek and were raising a new crop, oranges, in the late eighties and early nineties; Rosenbaum settled north of the township near the Trabuco and the Oso Creeks as far as Rancho Capistrano, which is today owned by the Schuller Ministries.

Farmers did not have it easy. Water was still a problem because rivers frequently diminished in size during the summer. The new farmers had to enlarge the existing zanjas (open water-ways) and incorporate new irrigation methods to get water to their crops. Marketing was also a problem. The population centers were still Los Angeles and San Diego although by the 1870s, there were markets in Anaheim, Santa Ana, and a few other small settlements. The coming of the railroad would partially solve this problem, although at great expense. But the first commercial farmers in the area had to haul their own products by wagon or sell to teamsters at a much lower price.

In 1875, the first map of San Juan Capistrano Township was recorded in the Los Angeles County Book of Records. It was done by E. R. Nicoles, surveyor, at the request of J. E. Bacon, Frank Riverin, and Father Jose Mut. Property owners, street names, and exact acreage figures were given. Many of the names on the map are families still prominent in San Juan. The street names, however, are greatly changed, showing a mixture of Californio

Tiburcio Vasquez was a bandit who supposedly gathered his men under sycamore tree north of town before raiding the town.
Courtesy of Dick Rambo

Shown here is Jose Juan Olivares, left, roping cattle. Jose Juan moved to San Juan in the 1850s as a small boy
Courtesy of the San Juan Capistrano Historical Society

and Yankee influences. El Camino Real from the southeast corner of the mission northward is called Main Street. Ortega Highway from Camino Capistrano to El Camino Real is called Broadway. Los Rios is Occidental; El Camino Real east of the plaza is called Oriental. The only street that retains the same name today is Spring, the street that runs from the east side of the mission near San Juan School.

Although San Juan had become a miniature melting pot, the Spanish language and culture still dominated the pueblo. In the memoirs of Jose Juan Olivares, a story is told about a fiesta called *La Fiesta de Ocho Dias*. This activity was held in June and was like a farmers' fair in which each farmer displayed the products from their gardens in little booths. A ceremony would follow in which a priest, followed by six small girls dressed in white, would visit each booth. The small girls would sing and strew petals along the way. Prizes were awarded to the best booths. After this ceremony, people in the town held a bullfight in the plaza. This would be followed by a feast in which all the food was donated by the people in the town. People from Los Angeles to San Diego would come for the barbecue. In the evening there was a fandango where dances with such names as La Jota, El Sombrero, La Contradanza, and El Borego were performed.

In later years, the town barbecue was held

on the Fourth of July and was given by Marcos Forster, son of John and Ysidora Forster. What was done to celebrate the American centennial is not known, but it was probably lauded in the usual way with a fiesta and barbecue, and perhaps a bullfight or bull game. Jose Juan Olivares recalled that the bull game, as opposed to the bullfight, was held in the mission quadrangle. A sack of coins was tied to the bull's horns and any enterprising person was welcome to try to get it. In this game, the bull's life was always spared but participants' lives were sometimes in danger. Non-native residents, writing in the 1890s, called the game "barbaric."

The town of San Juan, one year after the American centennial, was described in the *Los Angeles Herald* as having a schoolhouse, telegraph office, post office, two stores, a hotel, four saloons, and forty or fifty homes, mostly adobe. It also had a stage stop and a resident priest, Father Jose Mut. The school in 1877 was a wooden building constructed a few years earlier near the large pepper tree on Spring Street. Its forerunner had been a one-room adobe on the same site.

Records for the San Juan Elementary School District go back to 1854. It is believed to have been one of three schools operating in Los Angeles County in 1850. Early attempts at education had been made by the Franciscans, but the first government-affiliated school probably did not exist in San Juan until after statehood in 1850. Among first trustees of the district were Juan Avila, Juan Forster, and Manuel Garcia, according to records in the California Superintendent of Public Instruction's office. Meiton Hill in *100 Years of Public Education in Orange County*, noted that the first teacher in San Juan was T. J. Scully, who was paid one hundred dollars for three months of instruction. In 1855, when Santa Ana's school opened, the school board reduced his salary to seventy-five dollars because he taught three months in San Juan, then packed his saddlebags and rode off to teach three months in Santa Ana. It is interesting to note that Forster didn't send his children to public school, but maintained a tutor.

One thing San Juan did not have in 1876 was an organized fire department. If it had it might have saved the beautiful block-long hacienda of Juan Avila which was destroyed by fire in 1879. Avila, known as "El Rico," was the

grantee of Rancho Niguel in the early 1840s. He also owned a ten-room home on the west side of the town plaza, along what is today Camino Capistrano from the middle of the Franciscan Plaza to the two-story Casa de Garcia. According to historian Alfonso Yorba, the Valenzuela Adobe stood on the corner of Garden and Central (Verdugo and Camino Capistrano), but was joined by a common wall to a small adobe owned by the Pryors, which in turn was joined to the Avila home, giving the appearance of one long continuous building.

It was thus a shock to see flames shooting from the magnificent dwelling, lighting the sky for miles, fouling the air with the acrid smell of despair. According to eyewitness accounts, servants escaped the conflagration, but most of the valuable furnishings perished. Friends jumped on horses and lassoed ornate window shutters, dragging them from the burning walls and into the street. Others took the hinges off the great carved doors and carried them to safety. The

Juan Avila, "El Rico," was the original grantee of Rancho Niguel, and owner of the Avila Adobe.
Courtesy of the Los Angeles County Museum of National History

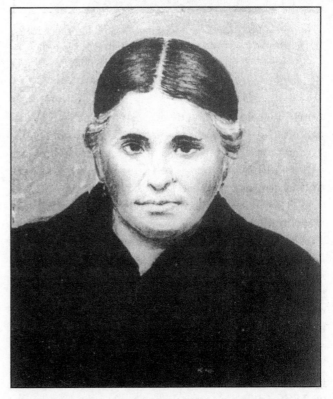

Soledad Yorba de Avila, the wife of Juan Avila, was a victim of smallpox epidemic of the 1860s.
Courtesy of the Los Angeles County Museum of National History

Henry George Rosenbaum settled in San Juan in 1869. He farmed the area where Village San Juan is today. Courtesy of Merle Rosenbaum Cannady

house was lost, but adobe walls stood, so Avila rebuilt the southern portion. He died in 1889. Today it still survives and is currently used for an office, although plans call for it to be restored and become a part of a restaurant.

The mission also survived at the end of the street but its endurance was an effort. Walls on the north and west sides of the quadrangle had caved in and mounds of debris threatened to invade the mission patio; lonely arches stood outlined against the sky, the only reminders of the height and form of the once-magnificent structure. Peacocks roamed the corridors, their anguished cries filling the night, as though mourning the loss of a loved one. The Franciscans were gone. The Forsters were gone. Only Father Mut was left, but even he would be gone by 1886 and no one would be sent to take his place. James Steele, who visited the mission in the early eighties, wrote this of the room used by Father Mut:

"By no possibility could any little chamber be more gloomy, unfurnished, generally dilapidated and desolate. A battered old pine table stood in the middle of the floor, and beside it a mended chair. Another, with a rawhide bottom stood beside the door. There was no whole glass in the one window and so the shutters were closed. An old and worn black priest's coat hung against the wall and the cheapest variety of cotton umbrella leaned beside it. An ecclesiastical book lay on a table where it had last been used, and close beside it a pair of steel-bound spectacles. The only sign of creature comfort, the one human weakness of the place, was a little bag of cheap tobacco and a wooden pipe that lay beside the spectacles and the book."

Such were the conditions under which the last resident priests had to function, yet the aura of the mission and tranquility of the town impressed the visitor, as it would countless others who would follow. Outsiders could already sense the uniqueness of San Juan, the impact of its past, and the role this would play in its future. In *Old California Days* published in 1889, James Steele recalled his visit and characterized the town:

"The peace which to some degree may come in life was never in this world nearer its idealization than in San Juan Capistrano three quarters of a century ago. It cannot be put into words, or painted, or sent by mail, but something of it broods there still. It is in the air, and to supplement it or add to it is the feeling that the past has not yet quite gone away."

Nor would it ever.

Seen here is a house built by Joel Congdon in 1877. Congdon started the English walnut industry in Orange County. His groves were near Alipaz and Del Avion, where his house still stands and is newly restored.
Courtesy of Mark Gibson

An early freight wagon hauled crops to distant markets. Wheat and barley were popular early crops in the valley.
Courtesy of the San Juan Capistrano Historical Society

The first official map of San Juan Capistrano was filed in 1875. The town was then part of Los Angeles county. Courtesy of the City of San Juan Capistrano

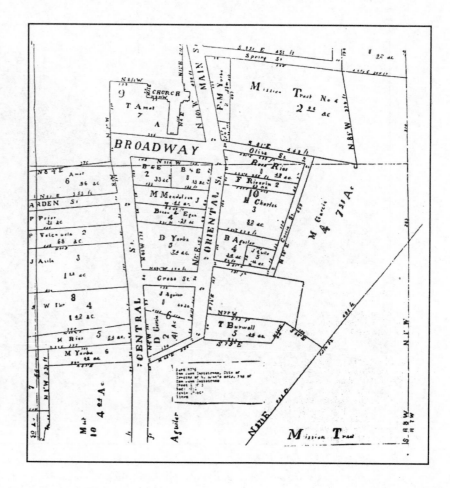

This view of downtown San Juan Capistrano from the mission looking south in 1888 shows Avila Adobe ruins. It burned in 1879, and only the southern portion was rebuilt.
Courtesy of the First American Title Insurance Company

This is a view of the mission ruins, looking east.
Courtesy of the First American Title Insurance Company

Here is an 1890s gathering at Pryor Adobe, formerly hides storage house. The Pryors owned Rancho Boca de la Playa.
Courtesy of the San Juan Capistrano Historical Society

The depot at San Juan-by-the-Sea, built in 1887, was similar to the original Capistrano Depot.
Courtesy of the First American Title Insurance Company

Chapter 4

Life in the Gay Nineties
1887 – 1900

The turn of the century, which could bring a new era of progress and a new way of life, came early to San Juan Capistrano. It began in 1887 when the California Central Railroad, a subsidiary of Santa Fe, began laying its tracks from Santa Ana to Oceanside, completing the last link in the coastal route and providing Capistrano with easy access to the rest of the economic world. While Americans focused on manifest destiny abroad and sampled the fruits of the industrial age, San Juan Capistrano in its own minute way felt the effects of these national themes. While remaining primarily an agrarian community, it now had a direct link with outside markets, outside culture, and what would someday become the mainstay of its economy — tourists.

The rancho period which had almost disappeared by 1880 in most of California lasted a little longer in Capistrano. Marcos Forster, son of Don Juan Forster, still played the role of the grand ranchero and retained many of the trappings of the romantic era though his ranch was much smaller than his father's had been and many newcomers with both large and small holdings surrounded him. Don Marcos was fond of huge barbecues to which all of Capistrano were invited, gay fiestas to celebrate birthdays, weddings, baptisms, and holidays, and spirited horse races, many of which he sponsored, right through the main streets of town. In 1883, he built a terracotta brick mansion at the southeast corner of El Camino Real and Forster Streets, which he called the Casa Grande. The house, which stood until 1964, was the setting for many of the town's social activities, all of which were provided free. Two views exist of Don Marcos — one is that of benevolent hospitable patron and the other is that of ruthless landowner. As an old-style ranchero, Don Marcos was probably a little bit of both. He was an anachronism, but in that respect symbolized San Juan Capistrano, which was an anachronism itself. Its contemporaries, Los Angeles and San Diego, spilled over their boundaries a dozen times, yet San Juan stood still. A new era came with the railroad, but it would develop slowly as though giving the town time to stretch and doze before having to wake up.

One of the first curiosities that came with the railroad was the depot. The first Capistrano depot was a large wooden building constructed in an almost Nordic style with ornate windows and scalloped roof pieces. The style was similar to other stations built by Santa Fe and its subsidiary companies at that time. The stop was called "Capistrano" on an 1891 schedule, with the "San Juan" stop being three miles further at San Juan-by-the-sea. A guidebook, published in 1888, however, referred to the station as "San Juan Mission." In 1891, the original wooden depot is mentioned in a booklet put out by the Santa Ana Board of Trade, but by 1892, there was already talk of replacing it with something more in the Mission style. Chief engineer Fred Perris wrote a letter to San Juan's Judge Richard Egan on October 21, 1892, telling him that he had received permission to build a new depot.

Construction did not begin the following spring, but a year after that in 1894. "Our new depot is progressing nicely. It will be finished in June when

Two men are seen here in mission ruins in 1880.
Don Dolores Yorba is shown with Gregorio Lopez, kneeling.
Courtesy of Alfonso Yorba

a grand ball will be given." This brief news item appeared in the April 14, 1894, edition of the *Santa Ana Standard*, a weekly paper that had a columnist from San Juan Capistrano. The writer was Dr. Alexander Hamilton Rowan, a transplanted Ohioan (brother-in-law of Santa Ana's founder, William Spurgeon), whose columns provide an interesting glimpse of life in San Juan during the Gay Nineties. Rowan does not mention the depot again until June 9, when he said the depot would soon be open and an excursion would be planned for Santa Anans on July 4. But in July of 1894, a crippling railroad strike halted all operations and when it was over Rowan wrote: "Old San Juan will soon blossom with the finest depot on the Santa Fe system. We invite the architecturalistic to come and view this unique building illustrated with arches, a dome 40 feet high with a mission bell, dainty ticket office, and quaint old-fashioned fireplace that will capture the tenderfoot as he breathes this balmy sea air." In spite of delays, the town held a celebration to herald the beginning of the new station, but the dancing and feasting were premature. On October 8, Rowan finally announced that the depot was finished. "Our old Aunt Sally of a depot had to go. It was torn down and converted into a fence to hide the unsightly side of Madrid Street from the eyes of those Eastern

beauties who go into hysterics over a beautiful background." Not only did the old depot become part of a fence, it also became part of a downtown building. Old pictures show the depot's distinctive windows on a store.

One immediate change that the railroad brought to Orange County was a land boom. Paper cities with schools, hotels, churches, and residential lots neatly platted sprang up overnight. Two opened near the mission community — Aliso City to the north and San Juan-by-the-sea to the south. The land boom, according to historians, can be traced both to active promotional campaigns designed to attract settlers and to a rate war between the Southern Pacific and the Santa Fe which began in 1885 and peaked in 1887. Glenn S. Dumke in his book *The Boom of the Eighties*, wrote that on March 6, 1887, the rate war centered on the fare between Kansas City and Los Angeles.

"Finally, shortly after noon, the Southern Pacific announced a rate of one dollar," wrote Dumke. But the madness was short. By March 10, the fare was again up to ten dollars. According to Steve Donaldson and Bill Myers in *Rails Through the Orange Groves*, the fare steadied at about twenty-five dollars.

The boom was over as quickly as it had started. Historian Don Meadows in *Orange County Under Spain, Mexico, and the United States,* notes that the boom collapsed because land prices were inflated, banks stopped loaning money on unimproved real estate, buyers waned, and new arrivals decreased. Towns failed to materialize, taxes made improvements a liability and mortgages came due. Aliso City survived to become the settlement of El Toro, but San Juan-by-the-sea, the place where society held picnics, attended dances, and Sunday bullfights, died.

Dr. Rowan wrote in August of 1894, "Those

La Casa Grande, built in 1882 by Marcos Forster, was the first terra cotta brick building in town.
Courtesy of the San Juan Capistrano Historical Society

who have seen San Juan-by-the-sea in its palmy days cannot bear to look at it now. Wrecks of the hotels, cottages and once-imposing depot are now in ashes and have marred the place beyond recognition. Stupid greed did it. Nothing is left standing but the water tank, the old Dutch Hall and an unsightly barn within the limits of the original townsite. It looks for all the world like a desert surrounded by a thousand graveyards." San Juan-by-the-sea would live again as Serra, then Doheny Park and Capistrano Beach. Today it is part of Dana Point.

While new cities prospered or died, San Juan Capistrano residents were beginning to assess the impact of the railroad on the economics of their community. Cattle and sheep, grain and even some perishable commodities (which had only short distances to travel) could now be sent directly to market from their own San Juan station. This cut costs and travel time.

To give an example of the productivity of the Capistrano Valley, Dr. Rowan presented these figures at the end of May, 1891: 225 tons of hay, one thousand quintals of wool, ten thousand mutton sheep, lambs, wegglers, and ewes, sixty-two tons of English walnuts, six cars of honey, six carloads of oranges, eight carloads of corn, three tons of dried fruit, three carloads of green apples, two tons of pears, and two thousand head of cattle from the Mission Viejo Ranch and two hundred head of horses. Rowan assured the reader that the figures were correct, but did not say what time they covered. From subsequent accounts, it appears that the figures were for the year.

"The walnut crop of this valley is immense and if the walnut connoisseurs of the famed Riviera and Malaga in the south of France could see our orchards they would yield the palm that the Capistrano Valley is the chosen paradise of the English walnut," wrote Rowan. The walnut industry, started by Joel Congdon in 1870, originated in San Juan Capistrano. According to Samuel Armor's *A History of Orange County*, Congdon's first yield was six thousand pounds which he drove by wagon to Los Angeles and sold for seven cents a pound. Walnuts continued to be one of the valley's primary crops until the late 1930s, when many were torn out and replaced with orange trees. Oranges, too, were already thriving in 1890. The largest and perhaps the only orange grower at that time was John Daneri. Rowan wrote about a visit to Daneri's orchards after a freeze. "We visited J. Daneri's orange orchard yesterday. We saw no scale, red, black or any other color. Although the crop is not so heavy this last year they make up in size and beauty. Mr. Daneri will begin shipping oranges in a few days to the San Francisco market." The orange industry, small at that time, began to be a major crop in the valley around 1914.

Cattle and sheep were raised in the hills behind the valley. Marcos Forster and Richard O'Neill were the major cattlemen of that period and Rowan's reports are filled with the numbers of "fat cattle" shipped by Forster and O'Neill to the markets of Los Angeles, San Francisco, and San Diego. Forster also had an interest in sheep, having at one time a partnership with Jean Daguerre. Daguerre went on to form a partnership with Lewis F. Moulton whose ranch encompassed much of Laguna Niguel, Laguna Hills, and El Toro. The sheep industry during the 1890s was dominated by Moulton and San Juan's Domingo Oyharzabal, who settled in Capistrano in 1878. The industry was so extensive that local labor couldn't handle it. Sheepshearers came annually from Temecula and Pala, their numbers reaching from sixty to eighty during the wool harvest.

Another major crop grown on the outskirts of town was wheat. The largest wheat grower was Aaron Buchheim whose acreage spread over the hills from Capistrano Beach to El Toro. Buchheim was also an inventor, creating many labor-saving tools for use on his ranch.

Industry in a limited form came to San Juan in 1890. A corporate concern headed by Belford and Company formed San Juan Capistrano's first full-scale manufacturing concern — the cannery.

It was with some excitement that Rowan announced in his columns early in 1890 the opening of the new cannery. "The events of the past week are very encouraging for Capistrano. The shining new redwood lumber looms up with grand effect as a fresh suggestion of the glorious future of this place. The cannery is 120 by 35 feet and built parallel with the railroad. The location is near the site of the new depot grounds and will be run by Mr. Hoyle, chief crystallizer, and Mr. James N. Wamersley of Norwich, England, two intelligent and energetic young gentlemen which speaks volumes for the success of this important enterprise. The farmers and horticulturists are taking in new life, and the conversations on streets and curbstones indicates that a new

The new Capistrano Depot opened in 1895. It was built more in the mission style.
Courtesy of the San Juan Capistrano Historical Society.

A threshing crew worked in the hills around San Juan Capistrano at the turn of the century.
Courtesy of the First American Title Insurance Company

impetus will be given to fruit growing in this favored region."

A glassware house was erected next to the cannery and plans were made for marketing the fig marmalade, dried fruit, and pickled olives which would carry the label "San Juan Brand." Plans for an olive oil factory were scuttled however when Santa Ana banks would not provide financing.

The cannery flourished for four or five years, but was apparently beset by problems. In 1896, it closed and by summer all of its equipment had been sold. The following year Belford announced he would reopen the cannery in the midst of his orchard (a mile east of town on the north side of the Ortega Highway). The new company would be called "Mission Brand" and would provide

summer jobs for idle youngsters. Nothing more was said about the new cannery and it isn't known if it was a success. If so, the success was brief because by 1910 the entire Belford estate had been sold to Father Alfred Quetu.

Despite the failure of manufacturing to take hold in the San Juan Valley (there had also been a brief attempt at starting a match factory), people continued to come to the area. The land boom, the railroad, and a very active Santa Ana Board of Trade (forerunner of the modern-day Chamber of Commerce) continued to encourage visitors, many of whom stayed. In 1891, the Board of Trade wrote optimistically that San Juan was "indeed a delightful section and will speedily become a thickly settled portion of the county."

While San Juan Capistrano's population was

Richard O'Neill purchased John Forster's ranchos in 1882 for
his partner, James C. Flood.
Courtesy of the San Juan Capistrano Historical Society

growing very slowly, other areas had blossomed. Feeling a new awareness of themselves and their potential, political leaders decided it was time to loosen their ties to Los Angeles County and stand on their own.

Attempts at county division had begun as early as 1870 when Anaheim Mayor Max von Strobel pushed a bill to create the new county of Anaheim. Over the next twenty years there were four more unsuccessful attempts using the name "Santa Ana County" in addition to "Orange County" which was selected because it evoked images of sea breezes, warm climate, and fertile soil — a Mediterranean atmosphere.

On January 14, 1889, when Col. Eugene E.

Edwards introduced "An Act to Create Orange County, to Determine its Boundaries and Seat, and to Provide for the Organization and Election of Officers," in the twenty-eighth Legislature, oranges were actually a very promising crop. Grapes, hogs, and sheep were more prominent crops, but none of those names were thought to be appropriate for the new county.

Supporters of the bill argued that the southern portion of Los Angeles County was not receiving its fair share of county services. Roads were unpaved, bridges were not built, and most county officers were from Los Angeles. It was also a very long way to the county seat.

There was fierce opposition from Los Angeles

businessmen and from the city of Anaheim. People in Anaheim had once hoped their town would become the center of county government, but boundaries had been redrawn just prior to the bill's introduction and moved to Coyote Creek instead of the San Gabriel River, making Anaheim too far north for the capital. The bill passed the Assembly on February 12, but had a more difficult time in the Senate. Edwards called for assistance in the form of William Spurgeon and James McFadden who, in the words of historian Jim Sleeper, "spread the largesse of the Santa Ana Valley where it would argue loudest." The amount spent is rumored to have been from $10,000 to $30,000. Whatever the amount, the job got done and on March 8, the Senate approved the bill, and three days later Gov. Robert Waterman signed it.

But it still had to be ratified at home.

Despite a campaign by Anaheim, the final vote count was 2,509 votes for and 500 against the

formation of Orange County. In San Juan, where the pros and cons were argued on street corners, at dinner parties and at wakes, the vote was 80 for and 16 against.

San Juan did not contribute greatly to the formation of the new county, but it did contribute some "firsts" to county annals. The first felony conviction recorded in the new county record book was a case involving a young San Juan woman whose name was Modesta Avila.

Historian Jim Sleeper described Modesta as a "dark-eyed beauty of San Juan" who depended more on her charms than her wits to keep food on the table and a roof over her head. She was also fiercely proud and willing to stand up for her rights. One of her opponents was the Santa Fe Railroad.

According to newspaper accounts in the Standard and Blade, Modesta claimed that the railroad had never paid her mother for right of way through her land (in northern Capistrano). Failing

Men came from Temecula and Pala to help shear sheep at a site located near Marco Forster Junior High today.
Courtesy of the First American Title Insurance Company

to get anyone interested in her cause, Modesta decided to take the matter into her own hands. They hadn't paid, so they were trespassing; they had no right to run their trains through her mother's property. Besides, the trains were noisy and dirty and kept her chickens from laying eggs.

With this logic at work, Modesta placed an obstruction across the tracks. Local storytellers claimed that it was nothing more than her Monday morning wash. But transcripts of the trial indicate it was something more substantial — a railroad tie.

Feeling remorseful, Modesta confessed to the local railroad agent who helped her remove the obstruction before the train was due. Nothing more was said or done.

But on October 15, 1889, four months after the incident took place, charges were filed against Modesta Avila who was taken to jail in Santa Ana. She was ordered to stand trial for attempted obstruction of a train, despite a plea for dismissal made by her attorney, George Hayford. Jurors were rounded up and on October 22, her trial was held. The jury tied, so the bail was reduced and a new trial was set for October 28. During the second trial, it was rumored that Modesta, an attractive, unmarried twenty-year-old, was pregnant. She was found guilty and was sentenced to three years in San Quentin.

Hayford filed several appeals and even wrote that his client had been convicted on the basis of her reputation, not her deed. He was able to get a hearing before the California Supreme Court on the issue that her crime had predated the formation of the county and she should not have been tried in an Orange County Court, but he lost on a technicality. Modesta Avila died after serving two years of her sentence.

Another first for Orange County was coroner's case number one — the murder of Henry Charles. Charles was a merchant who had come to San Juan Capistrano as a teenager, opening his first store just prior to the Flores incident of 1857. A prosperous businessman who had extended his holdings, he was shot on the night of August 24, 1889, while at home on his ranch two miles east of town. Charles had gone outside on that warm summer's night to take a stroll and enjoy a smoke in the evening air. He stopped in front of a shed to light his pipe when a shot rang out of the dark, striking him. Stumbling into the house he fell at the feet of his wife, sister-in-law, and a visitor. He said he did not know who had shot him and he died the next day.

After a brief investigation, authorities arrested his stepson, Emilio Loperu. It was well-known in the community that Charles and his stepson did not get along. Loperu, however, had an alibi for the night

Shown here is a steam tractor used on Aaron Buchheim's ranch at the turn of the century.
Buchheim farmed from El Toro to Capistrano Beach.
Courtesy of the San Juan Capistrano Historical Society

of the crime. He produced three women and two men who swore he was in bed at the time of the murder. The authorities released Loperu and began to look elsewhere.

A short time later — September 12 — a renegade called Silvestro Morales was arrested and accused of the shooting. Although there were no witnesses, it was established that Morales had been in the area on the night of the crime. He had also abducted and seduced a young girl from a prominent San Juan family, an act which shocked the community and the jury of "peers" from Victorian Santa Ana. He was convicted and given a life sentence.

San Juan had another spectacular murder nine years later. This one, too, was a shopkeeper whose name was J. Dolores Garcia.

"On Wednesday evening, Mr. Dolores Garcia, an old resident, was murdered in a cowardly manner," wrote Dr. Rowan. "He was standing in the door of his saloon when his assailant fired a bullet from a Winchester rifle, striking Garcia in the mouth and going through his head. Garcia died instantly. The perpetrator of the outrage is said to be a vicious half breed Indian who for years past has held a grudge against him and threatened to kill him."

And, in the judicious spirit of Victorian journalism, Dr. Rowan added, "If the assassin is tried on his looks he will stand but little show, for a more brutal looking wretch is hard to find."

The Indian's name was Manuel Feloros, also called "Mestizo" and he was convicted and ordered to hang. But after changing his plea to guilty, the judge did not sentence him to die, but to be imprisoned for life. Several years later he was released. He returned to San Juan where he worked on a ranch until he died. Rumors, still alive, claim that prominent citizens had ordered and paid for the murder in order to get Garcia's land. Some descendants of Garcia still believe this, but no others were ever charged.

Crimes in San Juan Capistrano weren't all violent. In November of 1896, the town was plagued with a transient problem, the favorite hangout being the cemetery. "Never in the history of this place has there been so many tramps," wrote an exasperated Dr. Rowan. "The tombs are full of them awaiting their destiny. Yesterday, four of them were led out from the tombs looking like living ghosts, to receive their sentences. And still the work of the merry policeman goes on."

People in San Juan had their share of deaths and perfidy to keep conversations going. But they also had some high times to talk about — particularly the occurrences at Harmony Hall.

Harmony Hall was the name given to the brick residence of Judge Richard Egan, which is still located on Camino Capistrano across from the El Adobe. Egan was a study in contrast. A serious school board trustee for thirty-two years, he was also a colorful character whose sense of humor still touches the town where he settled in 1868. Egan bought 160 acres in the north end of town near the confluence of the Oso and Trabuco creeks where he lived in an old adobe for years raising barley and other crops. He later bought six hundred acres east of the mission which he cultivated, and in 1883, he built his two-story brick home (using bricks left over from the construction of the Casa Grande the year before) and moved into town. Some historians claim that Egan was a self-appointed judge although historian Ellen Lee, an authority on Egan, states

Judge Richard Egan, shown with Lewis F. Moulton, came to the valley in 1868. He was once called the "King of Capistrano."
Courtesy of the San Juan Capistrano Historical Society

This steam tractor had a long belt to prevent sparks. Fire was a special danger,
since there was no organized fire department then.
Courtesy of the First American Title Insurance Company

that he was one of two justices of the peace for San Juan Township from about 1870 to 1890. An old story survives that his first election was to the post *juez de plano* (judge of the plains). It supposedly took place shortly after he manned a chuck wagon during a roundup. It is said that Egan dished out enough Irish charm along with the beans and tortillas so that during the next election he won. From then on he was known as Judge Egan, a title he held for life.

In the Gay Nineties, Judge Egan was the virtual "king" of Capistrano. And because he bore the title "king" (something he was dubbed by his close friend, actress Madame Helena Modjeska) he set about knighting all his friends. The Mendelsons, owners of a ranch and the Mendelson Inn, were the Duke and Duchess, and rancher and road commissioner H. G.

Rosenbaum was the Earl. Whenever columnist Rowan wrote about any of these people he frequently used their titles instead of their names.

An early plow used in Capistrano Valley is seen here.
Courtesy of the San Juan Capistrano Historical Society

One of the first industries in San Juan Capistrano was an 1890s cannery dispensing olives, dried fruit, and marmalade. It was located north of the depot on the west side of the tracks.
Courtesy of the First American Title Insurance Company

Historians joke about the "Free and Independent State of San Juan" having its own extradition policy with Mexico under the reign of Judge Egan. The origin of the story is that Egan once received a letter addressed to the *Presidente* of the Free and Independent State of San Juan Capistrano, asking him to extradite a criminal who was then living in Capistrano. Egan granted the extradition to Baja California and sent the man packing.

Though known for his blarney, Egan is also remembered as the person who was instrumental in getting the railroad through San Juan, who did much of the actual work on the mission restoration financed by the Landmarks Club in 1895, and who served as a Los Angeles County supervisor from 1880 to 1884. A surveyor by trade, he is remembered by some as scrupulously honest in all of his business dealings and by others as having an iron surveyor's chain for the poor and a rubber surveyor's chain for the rich. Whichever was the truth, Egan had a distinct and lasting impact on San Juan Capistrano and when he died on February 9, 1923, the town lost one of its most colorful citizens.

Egan was part of a small group of San Juan residents who were frequently mentioned in Rowan's columns, a group which dressed in the latest fashion, gave lavish dinner parties, and grand balls in their "mansions." Some of Rowan's accounts may have been slightly exaggerated to show the dandies in Santa Ana that San Juan was more than a sleepy little village with a crumbling mission. Yet they provide a glimpse of a different kind of lifestyle in the mission town, a lifestyle with European roots which fused with the Californio and emerged as a distinct facet of San Juan Capistrano culture.

The nineties in San Juan were gentle years, ones of prosperity and frivolity which, thanks to the Californio influence, never sank to the depths of Victorian gloom. In 1890, young ladies and gentlemen attended well-chaperoned picnics at San Juan-by-the-sea and danced under glittering chandeliers until morning. In 1894, San Juan had a cricket team which played against teams from Aliso City and Oceanside. That same year the Tansy Club was formed, a men's organization which gathered Indian artifacts and folklore, stored the paraphernalia in Harmony Hall, and frequently held public exhibitions. In 1897, light ties, yellow vests, tan shoes, and Peruvian hats were the rage for men while ladies wore dresses of fine lawn trimmed with ribbons and exchanged personal notes in delicate autograph books. There were grand balls given by the Forsters at Casa Grande, lavish dinner parties in the Mendelson and Pryor homes, card parties, concerts, piano and voice recitals, and art exhibits. Among those painting the mission was Madame Modjeska. H. G. Rosenbaum wrote a play called *Unique* which was produced in Los Angeles. A fiesta was held under the sycamores near Trabuco Creek. Carriages promenaded along the upper corso and along McKinley Avenue (Del Obispo).

One of the places Rowan admired most was Belford Terrace, a residence that was the scene of frequent social events. The Belfords owned the cannery, vacationed in Europe, and sent their daughter to a boarding school. When they moved to San Juan they bought the Morrow property on Valencia Rancho (on the north side of Ortega Highway) and built a huge Victorian mansion with towers and spires where a humble adobe once stood. When completed, Belford Terrace was one of San Juan's showplaces. It was lit by seventy-five gas jets and took two railroad cars full of furnishings to fill. It contained, according to Rowan, the "grandest collection of antiques, books, and paintings by great masters" and its library alone contained twenty-five hundred volumes.

The Belfords were gone by 1910. The cannery, beset by problems, eventually failed and the house was sold. The home's next owner was Father Alfred Quetu, a European of French extraction who came to San Juan with a colony of settlers, all of whom lived in the "old Belford place" as it was then called. The residents of the ranch drew a great deal of attention because of their beautiful Belgian draft horses and unusual ostrich farm. They didn't live there too long. On July 18, 1910, just thirteen days after he moved in, Father Quetu's Belford Terrace caught fire and burned to the ground. "Lightning had struck the top of the house about twenty minutes after six," wrote Father St. John O'Sullivan in his diary. "All were aroused and looked about, but could see no damage; however, after

Here is a label from an 1890s cannery. Notice the error in the mission's founding date.
Courtesy of Pamela Hallan-Gibson

The Orange County Courthouse in Santa Ana was the seat of government after construction in 1901.
Orange broke away from Los Angeles County in 1889.
Courtesy of the First American Title Insurance Company

some time, someone at a distance saw the top of the house on fire and gave the alarm. The gardener, Josef Guillmont, climbed up with an ax and tried to cut away the burning part, but failed to stop the fire and the whole house burned." It was never rebuilt.

While Belford Terrace was the epitome of sophisticated San Juan, a more raucous type of entertainment could be found downtown in what Rowan called "Forster's opera house." No one can remember which building was thus dubbed and Rowan failed to pinpoint its location, but it could have been the Casa Grande or the Woodmen's Hall or a two-story building on the corner of Verdugo and Camino Capistrano which had a store downstairs. Whichever building it was, the "opera house" contained an area for dancing, billiards, cards, and had rooms to let. It was a popular place to gather, especially on Saturday nights.

What should have been a relaxing event —

Modesta Avila was the first felony conviction in Orange County. She died in San Quentin after serving two years of her three-year term. She was convicted of attempting to obstruct a train.
Courtesy of Jim Sleeper

Pablo Pryor, a one-time owner of Rancho Boca de la Playa, died of strychnine poisoning. Courtesy of the San Juan Capistrano Historical Society

one head was broken; some got it in the neck and a tragic ending seemed imminent for awhile." The district attorney came to San Juan to prosecute the miscreants, but couldn't get enough information for a case, so he left and no one was jailed. If he had found someone willing to press charges, storing the accused villains would have been a problem. Having no overnight jail cell was causing problems even two years later when citizens decided to do something about it.

"One thing I would like to emphasize is that the great big guns of the county had better furnish our local officials the necessary means of discharging their duties or quit their abominable growling," wrote Rowan in January of 1896. "I refer to the establishment of a jail at this place. Our best citizens have taken the matter in hand and have submitted the matter to the proper authorities. Hereafter let the blame rest where it belongs."

County officials were not immediately receptive to the idea. Taking matters into their own hands, the residents of San Juan commissioned a local blacksmith to make their own jail cell. The Board of Supervisors then voted a small amount of money to build a structure to house the cell. In the November 28 issue of the *Standard*, Rowan wrote that the new jail and courthouse are nearing completion and would be an ornament to the upper corso. He does not, however, elaborate on the location, and we can only assume that the jail cell that oldtimers remember being on the west side of Camino Capistrano, near where the Trading Post is today, was the one built in 1896. It was relocated to the rear of the Combs residence and remained there for a number of years. Even with the addition of a new jail, the job of constable of San Juan Township was an unpopular one. County records show that between 1891 and 1910 there were eleven different men who held the job.

San Juan Capistrano was not a big town, but it experienced many visitors. Many of them passed through during the summer on their way to one of the most popular places in Southern California, a place discovered by Indians and translated into profits by Michael Kraszewski — the San Juan Hot Springs.

"Almost all diseases of a chronic nature are

the weekly concert — wasn't always. One, which took place in March of 1894, turned into a free-for-all typical of the rock concerts of the 1960s.

"Our weekly concert in San Juan was turned into a noisy festival and love feast in honor of Bacchus," wrote Rowan. "Blood flowed freely;

cured by a stay from three to six weeks at this thermal bathing place," wrote Rowan in 1897. "Drinking the water, too, will speedily work almost a miracle in rheumatism, skin disease, trembling nerves, uterine troubles of all kinds, indigestion and melancholia."

This place of miracles where water mysteriously bubbled from the ground was located twelve miles east of San Juan Capistrano. For fifty years it attracted campers, hikers, and bathers. Some came looking for peace and tranquility; others came looking for a miracle. What they found was fresh air, trees, and abundant wildlife, and 120-degree mineral water in which to soak away their troubles.

The hot springs were discovered by the Indians and shown to the padres who established the mission. Historians claim that the first recorded visit to the springs was in 1798 when a visiting priest from San Luis Rey spent some time in the healing waters. A mission station was set up at the agua caliente (hot water) rancheria and neighboring Indians treated for physical as well as spiritual ailments. Some historians believe the Sievers' adobe might have been this station. But Dona Lorenza Manriquez in an interview in the *Coastline Dispatch* newspaper shortly before her death in 1935, recalled that as late as the 1870s, an adobe existed near the main settling pools,

Miguel Parra Adobe is still standing today and is the home of the Capistrano Indian Council Museum.
Courtesy of the San Juan Capistrano Historical Society

with steps from the adobe leading down to the edge of one of the largest pools. By 1880, the adobe had crumbled and all but disappeared.

During San Juan Capistrano's pueblo years, many Mexican families used the springs, holding picnics and dances and even taking their wash. Some thought the hill behind the springs was haunted by the spirits of Indians who had died there, and would not venture further than the settling pools. Rancho Agua Caliente eventually became part of the Juan Forster holdings and was later sold to O'Neill and Flood as part of the sprawling Santa Margarita ranch. It was probably after this sale in 1883 that the resort was opened by Kraszewski, a friend of Juan Forster's, who retired from storekeeping in San Juan Capistrano to lease the springs and open a resort. In *California of the South,* a guidebook printed in 1888, the San Juan Hot Springs is listed as a flourishing resort which had by then been open for "several years." Travel to the springs had to be done by wagon until the opening of the railroad made it suddenly a convenient place to vacation.

"There are fine shade trees and a camping ground for all who can get there," wrote Dr. Rowan in 1890. "There's a good boarding house for those who don't want to do their own cooking. Rates are $5 or $6 per week.

Judge Richard Egan's Harmony Hall is seen here before fire destroyed the roof.
Courtesy of the San Juan Capistrano Historical Society

Every person must furnish his own bed and bedding and good tents can be hired on the grounds, cheap."

Visitors were told to take the train to San Juan Capistrano where they could hire a rig to bring them out for $1.00 to $1.50. Luggage was carried free.

One of the most frequent visitors to the area, and a man who probably helped popularize the springs in the nineties was the *Standard*'s editor, Dan Baker. Every

Judge Richard Egan's Harmony Hall after the roof was rebuilt.
The original second floor was destroyed in a fire in 1897.
Courtesy of the San Juan Capistrano Historical Society

Judge Richard Egan served as justice of the
peace from 1870 to 1890.
Courtesy of the San Juan Capistrano Historical Society

summer he visited the springs, but his biographer, Jim Sleeper, said he liked the camping rather than the soaking. In 1890, he wrote about the many things the atmosphere of the place could cure ... "violent temper, malignant disposition, fault finding, a desire for bloodletting and jealousy and worst of all, it actually usurps all feelings of remorse, a canker that may be lurking in the heart of the fairest flower."

Like Baker, most visitors came in the summer. Once he came in the fall and found another type of visitor:

"Tents are scattered through the woods and brush, but they are unoccupied except by hordes of cats which seem to multiply and grow and increase like the majority of the Republican returning board. The hungry, half-starved little nuisances make life a burden. They've stolen everything here in the meat line and have now started on my onions."

The hot springs bloomed. Soon Kraszewski, called Don Miguel, or just "Mac," added a store, dance hall, and a regular swimming pool. Later in the decade he added private cabanas containing shiny new bathtubs and individual cabins for people wanting a lengthy stay, but who didn't

These are visitors to Judge Egan's home in the 1890s.
The center person is Madame Helena Modjeska, the famous Polish actress.
Courtesy of the San Juan Capistrano Historical Society

eration to Ferris Kelly. Kelly operated the springs until 1936 when he suddenly closed the resort, sold all the buildings, and ended a colorful chapter in the history of San Juan Capistrano.

"Coming as a surprise and shock to the community this week was the announcement from Ferris F. Kelly that the Capistrano Hot Springs, one of the most popular health resorts in Southern

want to pitch a tent on the campground. Not only did folks come to soak and drink the hot mineral water, they also came to fish, hunt, play cards, and swap stories. Baker told about visiting preachers who sold religion, and visiting mediums who tried to rouse the spirits of the dead through open-air seances. It was a place of fun and frolic, marred only by the faces of those who came to be cured, those with "stiff legs, swollen joints, contracted muscles and, most melancholic of all, those with the tired out look from overwork and study who have aged prematurely."

The activity at the springs came to an end for Mac in 1902 when his lease was not renewed. Although the details have not been preserved, an article in the *Santa Ana Blade* noted that Kraszewski had become "inefficient." He also had become crippled in a riding accident and, unfortunately, the magic waters could not work their miracles on him. He returned to San Juan and died eight years later in a county home in Santa Ana.

Although Mac left, the springs survived under a number of proprietors. A popular one was Leon Eyraud who had the resort from the twenties until 1933 when he turned over the op-

Madame Helena Modjeska, was a frequent visitor at
Harmony Hall, the home of Richard Egan.
Courtesy of the First American Title Insurance Company

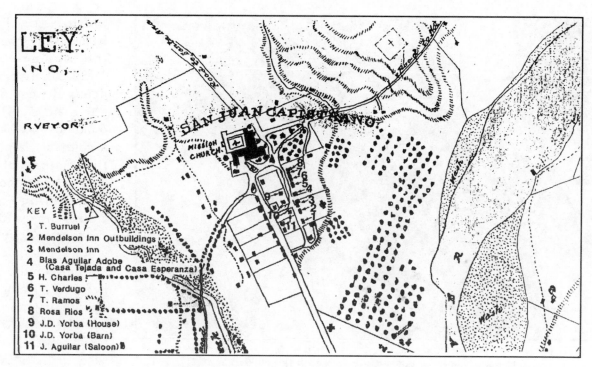

An 1888 map of San Juan Capistrano is seen here.
Courtesy of the City of San Juan Capistrano

Here is a view of El Camino Real looking north in the 1890s.
Courtesy of the San Juan Capistrano Historical Society

California, is nought but a memory," reported the *Coastline Dispatch* on October 9, 1936. Kelly told the reporter that he couldn't get a satisfactory lease and that all equipment at the resort was offered for sale including seventy-five buildings, fifty-eight cabins, one store, pavilion, bathhouse, dining room, and dance hall. In later issues it was reported that all the buildings were moved into San Juan Capistrano where many of them were renovated or disassembled for the wood. Some, like the dance hall (now a Senior Citizens Center), still stand in San Juan. According to historian Jim Sleeper, the real reason for the closure of the resort was a problem with the health department, which was going to require costly sanitation improvements. Despite this, efforts were made from 1936 to 1940 to obtain the resort as a place to treat polio victims, similar to Warm Springs, Georgia. According to published reports, the

U.S. government offered to buy it and add it to Cleveland National Forest, but the price was too high. It was later sold to Gene Starr and became part of the Starr Ranch until purchased by Orange

Lupe Combs House, built in 1878 in Forster City, was moved to San Juan in 1882. It is still standing on Verdugo Street today.
Courtesy of the San Juan Capistrano Historical Society

Belford Terrace, built in the 1890s, was later the home of Father Alfred Quetu.
Courtesy of the San Juan Capistrano Historical Society

Rancho Santa Margarita y Las Flores ranch house and bunk house. Now Camp Pendleton Commanding General's house.
Courtesy of the San Juan Capistrano Historical Society

Indians once thought Hot Springs were haunted by the souls of Indians who had gone there to die.
Courtesy of the San Juan Capistrano Historical Society

San Juan Hot Springs could cure any ill in the 1890s. It was located twelve or thirteen miles east of town.
Courtesy of the San Juan Capistrano Historical Society

Hot Springs Dance Hall was cut into three parts and moved into town were it became a duplex on Camino Capistrano. L'Hirondelle is there today.
Courtesy of the San Juan Capistrano Historical Society

County in the early 1970s. Today it is part of Ronald W. Caspers Regional Park, and was operated briefly as a resort by Russell Kiessig, until it closed.

The old springs are now in ruins, the cabins and tubs long removed, the place haunted by the laughter of revelers and the faces of invalids who came for fifty years. But the hot springs, perhaps more than anything else, signified the changes that took place in Capistrano during the Gay Nineties. Overnight it changed from a quiet, out-of-the-way place, to a busy, prosperous crossroads; a place people would return to — over and over again.

Ruins of the mission quadrangle were stabilized by the Landmarks Club in 1895.
Courtesy of the San Juan Capistrano Historical Society

Chapter 5

Progress and Mission Restoration
1900 – 1920

When the clocks struck 12:00 on the night of December 31, 1899, the American people were enjoying a period of prosperity. They had won their brief war with Spain, had expanded their influence beyond their boundaries, and had begun a period of self-examination which would be labeled the Progressive Era. The first few years of the twentieth century were marked by a crackdown on giant monopolies, a nationwide crusade for social justice, and an acceptance of rapid advance in technology. And though San Juan Capistrano would indirectly feel the effects of the first two themes, it was the third that would have a lasting impact on the oldest village in Orange County.

The mission was empty, its pillars licked by curling tendrils of weeds, its unroofed walls melting into piles of mud; sheep grazed in its courtyard and swallows nested in the cracks of the Great Stone Church. Yet its influence had not diminished. Abused by pillagers needing rocks and tiles, it still stood, a symbol of strength possessing the will to survive. It had structure and form when it should have been rubble; it had beauty, when it should have repelled. Time and indifference tore into it year by year, eroding its dignity, yet it retained its spiritual fascination, and people still came from miles around to pray among its ruins.

"The mission buildings on one side of the immense quadrangle dominate the view of the town as completely as they do also the thoughts of the townsfolk and visitors alike," wrote Odell Shepard in *Overland Monthly*. "For San Juan is one of the too few towns in America, the importance and significance of which is due to what they have been rather than what they are or may become."

Shepard remarked that the town's point of view was distinctly Spanish, yet distinctly its own. "One gains a new respect for the concentrated energy and the personal power and devotion of the padres when he sees how their influence prevails after all the years over the alien populations that they gave their lives to serve." And it was refreshing, he continued, to see that the most enduring monument was in human lives rather than brick and stone.

This view of San Juan symbolized the struggle that had taken place throughout the town's history — its desire to be unique and self-sufficient and small, while these very qualities acted as a magnet to draw people to it, people with different ideas and outlooks. One such group came in 1895 and their goal was to finance some changes. They were the Landmarks Club, a Los Angeles based organization which sought to preserve the missions of California, focusing on San Diego, San Juan Capistrano, San Fernando, and Pala.

"It is no exaggeration to say that human power could not have restored these four Missions if there had been five years' delay in the attempt," wrote the club's president Charles F. Lummis in *Out West* magazine.

The preservation of Mission San Juan Capistrano's existing structures was their first project. They re-roofed the buildings of the quadrangle that were still standing with tiles and re-paved 5,250 feet of walkways with asphalt and

Weed-choked corridors were all that remained of the once proud mission.
Courtesy of the San Juan Capistrano Historical Society

Visitors had always come to the mission. Franciscans, overland travelers, traders, sailors, miners, and settlers — anyone needing shelter for the night was welcome. But from the time Juan Forster vacated the mission, it had drawn another kind of visitor, the kind that walked through its grounds and examined its ruins and dreamed of the life that once went on within its walls. During the 1890s, more of these visitors came and in the summer of 1897, Dr. Alexander Hamilton Rowan wrote, "Lady tourists fill San Juan. They can be found in every nook and corner of the mission." Tourists came not only to wander, but to paint and photograph. Many stayed overnight or for longer, buying supplies at the general stores, taking their meals at the Mendelson Mission Inn where they could get served if they provided three hours' notice. Before its closure in 1903, visitors could stay at the French Hotel on Camino Capistrano, but between 1903 and 1918 the Mendelson was the only hotel in town.

The Mendelson was the destination of a unique group of tourists who came by train one rainy night in March 1910, pulling their three railroad cars onto the siding at the Capistrano Depot. According to an account by historian Jim Sleeper in *Shot in Orange County*, the occupants of the cars were employees of Biograph Studios who had arrived to film, the first film ever made in Orange County. Among them was the director, a hawk-nosed man who would become a giant in the film industry, and his leading lady, a diminutive seventeen-year-old with a heart-shaped mouth. Their names were D. W. Griffith and Mary Pickford.

The Biograph production crew took over the old Mendelson Inn in San Juan Capistrano. For three days the rain continued, and the shooting could not

gravel. They also provided the southwesterly building with a shake roof and repaired rents in the adobe walls. They secured what was left of the Great Stone Church, removed four hundred tons of debris, and installed an irrigation system for the garden area. Reassured that the remaining buildings would stand for a few decades more, the club then left Capistrano and turned its attention to another project. Because of the work of the Landmarks Club, there was now something more to see in San Juan Capistrano. The project had been well-publicized and many came to see what had been accomplished.

In 1895, the Landmarks Club reroofed existing buildings in the mission. This view is westerly toward "Little Hollywood."
Courtesy of the San Juan Capistrano Historical Society

terest soon turned to dismay. The crowd, not knowing anything about the script, thought the actors were mimicking the funeral of the day before and became very angry. They surged forward toward the actors and the crew, who ran for the safety of the hotel.

Mr. Griffith had not foreseen this problem and had to rely on the hotel proprietor to explain the scene to the mob and calm everyone down. He also volunteered to have his cowboys (who were former rodeo performers) put on a riding and roping exhibition, which pleased the

begin. The crew sat around with nothing to do while the director paced and checked weather reports. The only diversion was a traditional San Juan funeral procession which passed by the hotel on foot en route to the cemetery.

The next day the sun came out, the actors left the hotel in colorful early California costumes (it was a period film), and the first scene was shot — an Easter procession on its way to the mission. Interested in the activities, a large crowd gathered, but in-

Lady tourists filled every nook and cranny of Great Stone Church in the 1890s. Coming of the railroad made it easier for tourists to visit the mission.
Courtesy of the San Juan Capistrano Historical Society

Mendelson Hotel, built in 1875, was later remodeled. It was located on El Camino Real, South of Ortega.
Courtesy of the San Juan Capistrano Historical Society

crowd and allowed filming to resume.

Silent filmmakers returned several times over the years to use Capistrano as a setting, followed by those making "talking" pictures. One of the most memorable of the silent films made in San Juan was Douglas Fairbanks' *The Mark of Zorro*. Adapted from a magazine article by Johnston McCulley, the original name of the story was "The Curse of Capistrano."

New technology of the early twentieth century would soon make changes in the town. Writers, as well as filmmakers, had discovered the "quaint old Spanish town" and would soon be extolling its virtues in national magazines. Prosperity had put money in peoples' pockets, money for frills like vacations.

The town that tourists saw in 1914 was still a small farming community. Standing at the mission entrance looking south, on the east side of the street, would be a building marked saloon, a general store with a tall flagpole, a schoolhouse (moved from Spring Street to its new location in 1912 where it was converted into a restaurant), a livery and feed stable, another store that would be converted into living quarters for employees of the not-yet-built Palms Cafe, a vacant area, and the Egan home.

The west side of the street would contain a store owned by Landell and McCarty, another store facing Garden (Verdugo), a two-story building that would contain a store on the bottom floor, a one-story structure which would become the first telephone office, and a recreation hall first built as a church. Next to that was the remains of the Avila Adobe, now occupied by dressmaker Magdalena Murrillo, the two-story French Hotel, the Oyharzabal residence, the

A turkey destined for a cooking pot strolls behind Mendelson Inn. Early hotels raised their own poultry and vegetables for their restaurants.
Courtesy of Alfonso Yorba

This wooden school with the bell tower, built in the 1870s, is shown after its
move to downtown in 1912, where it was converted to a restaurant.
Courtesy of the San Juan Capistrano Historical Society

ductivity of the Capistrano Valley:

"John and Frank Forster, descendants of Don Juan Forster, who became owner of the mission in the forties, have a splendid property, stretching from the water montes beside the ever-flowing San Juan Creek far beyond the huge hills on the south side of the valley. Of their 3,500 acres, 2,000 is farmed, most of it to grain, this last year a little of it to that ever-increasing crop, lima beans."

Vanderleck Home (El Adobe), and another small adobe (now gone).

Surrounding the town were groves of walnut trees. "Descending from the thirsty, sun-baked hills into this green orchard country seemed to us, after our long tramp, like entering the promised land," wrote a visitor in 1915. Entering the town on foot from the hills that separated San Juan from Laguna, the visitor noted that there were walnut orchards dominating the entire valley; some trees were so old that although planted a hundred feet apart no sunlight penetrated the canopy of branches.

Outside of town were the spreading ranch lands of Frank and John Forster (sons of Marcos Forster), Cornelio Echenique, and Domingo Oyharzabal. Beyond that was the huge O'Neill Ranch, which spread from Oceanside to El Toro. A writer in *Harper's* magazine described the pro-

The writer noted that Echenique had quit the sheep business and had devoted 10,500 acres to cattle. He had subleased 4,000 acres that year, 3,300 for the growing of grain and 700 for lima beans. Domingo Oyharzabal had also given up sheep and had turned to cattle on his 2,000 acres.

"In the Trabuco the finest ranch is that owned by C. C. Crookshank, water from the Trabuco furnishing all that can be used in the maintenance of thriving groves of oranges, walnuts and fruits.

Horse racing was a popular sport in 1912. Races were held on Camino Capistrano.
Courtesy of the San Juan Capistrano Historical Society

Frank and Ada Forster are seen here on horses. Frank was the grandson of John Forster, who bought the mission in 1845.
Courtesy of the San Juan Capistrano Historical Society.

From out of this valley the trains carry no less than 120 carloads of grain per year, along with 20 carloads of beans and 35 carloads of hay."

Water was always a problem for farmers, but because of the existence of two good-sized streams (before upstream drilling reduced their size) water could be diverted to irrigation ditches (called zanjas) in the same method that mission fields had been irrigated during the Spanish period. When more settlers came to the valley two cooperative water companies were formed, one for each river, so that water could be distributed fairly. The Capistrano Water Company governed the main ditch that fed from San Juan Creek. The ditch, called the Mission Vieja ditch on the company's map filed in 1883, was a dirt channel, later cement, that followed the course of what is today the Ortega Highway, from its juncture with San Juan Creek. The other cooperative was the Trabuco Water Company whose ditch fed off Trabuco Creek. In the early part of the twentieth century those wishing water were

allowed one hour per acre per month. As the water came down the ditch, the person whose turn it was would place an obstruction in the path of the water, damming it and diverting it onto his own property for the prescribed length of time. A huge bulletin board was posted downtown with the month's schedule. Would-be violators thought twice before they stole the Capistrano Valley's most precious commodity. William Stroschein, Jr., a small child in San Juan at the turn of the century, recalled seeing men beaten with shovels and half-drowned in the stream for daring to divert water when it wasn't their turn.

In the *Harper's* article, the writer noted that at that time each person was allowed use of water every seventeen days. He admired the practice and said "no more efficient system is to be found in all California."

Around 1910, a group of French colonists settled in San Juan Capistrano. They were brought by Father Alfred Quetu, himself a native of France,

*A 1900 view of the original home of Frank and Ada Forster off
Ortega Highway, where Ortega Center is today.
Courtesy of the San Juan Capistrano Historical Society*

who bought five hundred acres on the north and south sides of what is today the Ortega Highway, much of which was the old Belford place. His farm is best remembered by old-timers because of the ostriches and horses raised there. One of his horses, Champlin, a 2,200-pound draft stallion, took first place in a special horse show, beating 159 contenders in Salt Lake City. His ostrich farm, which boasted sixty birds, was still thriving at the time of the *Harper's* article. But his luck didn't hold. After he lost two houses to fire, his group moved across the street and eventually dispersed to places of their own. According to Father Engelhardt, Father Quetu was attached to the mission from 1910 to 1914, but his greatest contribution to the town was in a chance meeting he had in Arizona in 1909 with a young priest suffering from tuberculosis whom he invited to visit San

Juan Capistrano. His name was St. John O'Sullivan.

The mission was still unrestored when Father O'Sullivan stepped off the train and walked slowly to the comer of Garden and Central (Verdugo and Camino Capistrano) and looked fully at the magnificent ruins surrounded by a rundown picket fence. He was captivated by the place and decided to stay, becoming the first resident priest of Mission San Juan Capistrano since 1886.

"Within the man burned a deep spirituality, a forceful flame that was fanned by his disease; he had no hope of living, he had no fear of death," wrote his biographer, H. Bedford-Jones. "Here awaited him overgrown and forgotten graves. Only the works of the Landmarks Club had saved the ruins of the mission from total obliteration. The place appealed to him; it was like himself, whose

*Here is the 1910 home of Frank and Ada Forster, the first stucco
house in Orange County. It is still standing on Ortega Highway.
Courtesy of the First American Title Insurance Company*

The Echenique House, now Four Oaks Park, was the home of
Mr. and Mrs. Cornelio Echenique, who are shown with Bonifacio Lacouague.
Many Basques were prominent in the community.
Courtesy of the San Juan Capistrano Historical Society

greatly admired the work of Father Serra. One of the first things he did was erect a statue to Serra's memory. It was dedicated August 13, 1914, and for a time stood at the front entrance, but was later moved to the position it holds today near the mission bells.

Many successful fund-raising activities took place during Father O'Sullivan's time. According to historians, among those aiding in the restoration were Walter Knott, Fred H. Rupell, Goodsun Borgland, and Roger B. Sherman, who laid out walkways and designed the fountains. Most of the trees and flowers were planted during this period. One pepper tree, near what is today the museum and gift shop, was supposedly planted in 1871 from a seedling obtained from the large pepper owned by the Oyharzabal fam-

body was gone in decay."

Like others before him, Father O'Sullivan was deeply impressed by the mission's survival against all odds. Through the next few months he carefully explored his new home and was fascinated not only by what it had been, but by what it could be.

"Ruined and despoiled and apparently useless as it was, the old mission had endured above those who had laid it low," wrote Bedford-Jones. "In itself it had been and was a vision and only where there is no vision do the people perish."

Father O'Sullivan supplied that vision, restoring not only the mission but also, miraculously, his own health. Guided by old stories and legends and materials it hand, he set to work making beams by hand and carving and mortising window frames. As things were uncovered he would store them for future use, and as the work progressed, more and more people came forward to lend a hand. His major concern was Father Serra's chapel, which had been reroofed by the Landmarks Club but was still in need of interior repair. To help fund the project, he initiated the donation made by visitors at the mission entrance.

Longtime residents of San Juan remember Father O'Sullivan as a patient, gentle man who

Father St. John O'Sullivan came to San Juan Capistrano
in 1910. His dream was to restore the mission and
he saw it fulfilled before his death in 1933.
Courtesy of the San Juan Capistrano Historical Society

ily behind the old French Hotel.

As the shrubbery grew, so did the number of tourists. Gasoline pumps began appearing in the downtown area. A few more eating places opened. San Juan Capistrano began to feel the effects of outside money spent in its places of business. Long-time residents recall this period — the second decade of the twentieth century — as San Juan's decade of progress. Most of the advancements were technological — electricity, telephone, and paved streets. Carl Romer, secretary to Jerome O'Neill of the Santa Margarita Ranch from 1910 to 1920, came into town two or three times a week. Because he was then a visitor, he paid attention to changes and recalled that the first experience with electricity came around 1913, when the old Fairbanks-Morse generator was installed where the former Edwards Cinema buildings are today.

"It was powered by a gasoline engine," he recalled. "A man would start it in the evening when the sun went down and would turn it off around 9:00 o'clock."

Later a small power plant was built by Edison on the then-outskirts of town north of the mission. San Diego Gas and Electric took it over in 1918 when a 75-mile transmission line was strung all the way from San Diego. Romer recalled that the Santa Margarita Ranch, which had its own battery-operated generator, obtained a line from the San Diego firm in exchange for right of way through their land. This was a much better system for the ranch because their old generator's batteries had to be charged every day.

Telephone also came into use around this time. Judge Egan was one of the first to have a phone installed in his home, a phone which was connected to the O'Neill Ranch. The ranch had its own phone system which was battery operated and stretched thirty miles. Each connection had its own series of rings which determined which phone should be answered. The first telephone operator in San Juan Capistrano was Fidel Sepulveda, who operated the Home Telephone Company in 1917. Because of right-of-way problems, callers were confined to the immediate area at first, then a connection was made to Elsinore and Riverside for those who wanted to call outside the area. A line was eventually obtained along the coast, but phones were not common for many years. Most people who wanted to make a call drove downtown to the office to make it, and if

The Landmarks Club shored up existing arches in 1895. Judge Richard Egan directed much of the work.
Courtesy of the San Juan Capistrano Historical Society

A view is seen from the mission entrance looking south in 1912.
Note the picket fence around the mission grounds.
Courtesy of the San Juan Capistrano Historical Society

Pete and Salvadore Labat's meat market on Camino Capistrano, where the Franciscan Plaza is today. C. Russell Cook, interviewed in 1975 at the age of eighty-one, recalled when a person could get a chunk of round steak at Labat's store for twenty-five cents. Food was cooked in wood-burning stoves or in primitive outdoor ovens and fireplaces, unless it was barbecued over an open fire. Some people had their own wells, but most people relied on the rivers for water. Those who did not were able to obtain water from the Oyharzabals, who were very generous with their well, later starting the first downtown water service.

a call came in for someone not immediately available, the operator would wait until the person came to pick up his mail and would give the message.

Despite the rapid progress that came after 1910, most residents still lived much like their parents had. Most people still used coal-oil lamps or gaslights. Many of the homes were of adobe, though most of these had been renovated and reroofed for protection against wind and rain. Other homes were of board and batten, some of them containing only one or two rooms, while others were of gracious proportions, such as the Albert Pryor house, which is now the O'Neill Museum. Only a handful were made of brick or stucco. Most people raised their own food; vegetables were grown in backyard garden plots, and fruit trees were found in every yard. Staples such as flour, sugar, and beans were purchased from downtown merchants, but many raised their own chickens and pigs for meat and had their own cows for dairy products. Those who could afford it bought their meat from

Outhouses were provided for sanitation. They also provided some amusement. Mrs. Delfina Manriquez de Olivares, a teenager in 1910, described the Judas Day activities (Saturday

Church services were held in the mission gift shop building, the former Forster living quarters, prior to restoration of Serra Chapel in the 1920s.
Courtesy of the San Juan Capistrano Historical Society

before Easter) popular at that time. According to Mrs. Olivares, the youngsters of the town would gather as many outhouses, wagons, and farm tools they could and would stack them against the walls of the mission. Some even found their way onto the mission roof. Then they'd hold a dance and hang the effigy of Judas. Sometimes it took farmers a week to remove and replace their outhouses and wagons, but in those days that was considered "good clean fun."

The Judas Day celebration was also popular in the Gay Nineties. Dr. Rowan described the activity in 1894: "Judas Day, so called, a curious barbaric custom among the natives here, took place on the 24th of March. The night previous, vehicles, grindstones, and everything movable was piled up against the mission where a grotesque image of Judas is placed on the unsightly pillars of stolen goods, where it remains until the afternoon of the next day when the great roar of commotion sets in and Judas is placed in a most undignified manner on a bull's back.

Ramon Yorba Adobe was located on El Camino Real, center.
Courtesy of the San Juan Capistrano Historical Society

The bull is then turned loose and makes a dash for the crowd of tormentors. The crowd hisses and yells and shouts of horror reach the climax of confusion; enough to make Judas turn in his grave or burst the tomb and smite these merry revelers."

The celebration apparently died out with the advent of indoor plumbing and a high mission wall. But the fun-loving kids of San Juan apparently didn't lack amusements. Barbecues were still very popular, as were dances, most of them held in a curious old building on the west side of what today is Camino Capistrano. The structure, which resembles an old church in pictures, was in fact built as a Protestant church.

In his January 4, 1896 column, Rowan mentioned that the "new union church is now nearly completed and a very handsome structure it is, too; another evidence of San Juan's pluck and enterprise. It is safe to say that San Juan erected more buildings this year than any town in the county, aside from Santa Ana." The church was used by "a little band of Baptists" but was not

Home Telephone Company, left, started in 1917. It and Labat's Meat Market occupied space in rebuilt portions of Avila Adobe where Franciscan Plaza is today. Courtesy of the First American Title Insurance Company

ued to use it for services as did organizations such as the International Order of Woodmen. Some people remember the building only as "Woodmen's Hall." One of the other amusements offered in the building was the showing of movies, but when this occurred, the structure had been moved again slightly to the northwest so that it could be reached from Verdugo. In 1919, Protestants of the community built a permanent church on El Camino Real opposite the east side of the mission. It is still in use today, start-

Here is a view of San Juan Capistrano looking south about 1911.
Note the picket fence in front of the mission. The Blue Goose packing house,
in background.
Courtesy of the San Juan Capistrano Historical Society

available to the group of Mormons who held services in town, something that Rowan thought was a terrible injustice. For some reason the church did not survive solely as a place of worship. By 1911, it was moved from its original location, approximately where the library is today, to the place where the Provincial Building stands today and was used for a variety of activities. Allen Henry Wright, who visited San Juan in 1911, was intrigued by the building:

"It is said that once some Protestant denomination established a small church outside of town," he wrote in *Overland Monthly*, "But it did not succeed in its work and today the structure, which was built is pointed out on the main street as the scene of dances and other amusements."

Protestants contin-

ing as a non-denominational community church, becoming a Presbyterian church and finally, a Christian church.

Education was another concern. The old wooden schoolhouse, built in the 1870s, had become overcrowded, so it was sold and moved and

Seen here is a view looking south over the town from Mission Hill in 1896.
The building in the foreground was a protestant church, later moved.
The library occupies the former church site today.
Courtesy of Alfonso Yorba

a new school was built around 1912. The new structure was the same architectural style as the depot, but it had two bell towers, instead of one. It lasted until the present-day San Juan School, which still stands today on the corner of El Camino Real and Spring Street, was built in 1964. The little schoolhouse of the 1870s was renovated first into the Palms Cafe, then the Bird Cafe, and was finally torn down with the restaurant in 1937.

Seen here is the rear view of buildings facing east on Camino Capistrano, around 1915. A baseball game is taking place where the movie theatre is today.
Courtesy of the San Juan Capistrano Historical Society

The schools at the turn of the century only went as far as the eighth grade. Those who wanted higher education had to go to Santa Ana and board with a family during the school year.

Santa Ana was also the only place you could get a doctor. San Juan had two doctors at the turn of the century. Dr. Rowan, the columnist of the 1890s, was not practicing because of retirement and Dr. Isadore Simard, also elderly, was more interested in the occult than medicine. Most people had to rely on themselves and remedies that had been handed down from generation to generation. Most of the remedies came from nature — roots, herbs, leaves, and sunshine. Some were skilled in natural medicine; others were not so fortunate, but could always find someone to advise them. Elderberry blossoms were considered good ingredients in a medicinal tea which generally kept you fit; sliced raw potatoes applied to the forehead could ease a headache. A poultice made from raw onions could be placed on one's chest to treat severe respiratory conditions, and hot lemon juice and honey was considered a universal remedy for coughs. Spider web could be used as an emergency blood

William McPherson, center, taught at San Juan School in 1910. The building is the second San Juan School, dating from the 1870s. The First was an adobe.
Courtesy of the First American Title Insurance Company

Workmen constructing San Juan School, which stood from 1912 to 1964. School records date back to 1854. Courtesy of the San Juan Capistrano Historical Society

ing to *Saddleback Ancestors*, a publication of the Orange County Genealogical Society, and was the daughter of an early mission carpenter, Tomas Gutierrez, who was also a grantee of land in 1841. In 1850, at the age of twenty-one, Polonia was already a widow. The census for that year noted that she was living with her parents in the home of her sister and brother-in-law, Mr. and Mrs. Blas Aguilar, on El Camino Real and her name was Montana (now referred to as Montanez). Her widowhood was short lived, however, as she fell in love with Francisco Canedo, who lived up the street and married him in an elaborate ceremony in the mission

coagulant and plants called lantana and jack rabbit ear were good for treating cuts. But if none of those things worked, one could always consult an Indian whose knowledge of herbal medicine was considered far superior. One Yaqui Indian woman from Mexico who was consulted in emergencies was called Doña Bernarda. She lived near Trabuco Creek in a house that had shelves lined with jars containing an assortment of herbs and plants. Though modern medical men would shudder at the pigs that lived under her bed and the dogs and cats that had free run of her home, she was able to cure many people who are still alive to tell about it. People didn't just see her if they had a cold, they also consulted her about love potions, the casting of spells (or undoing the effects of one), and unwanted pregnancies. Some people thought she was a witch and stayed away from her. Others went to see her, even though they were afraid, because they thought her powerful. Doña Bernarda eventually moved from San Juan, but her memory still lingers.

Babies, during the first two decades of the twentieth century, were born at home in San Juan Capistrano. Several women served as midwives, but one that is best remembered for more than just her midwifery skills was Dona Polonia Montanez.

Polonia was born Apolonia Gutierrez, accord-

Luis Cojo paints a grave marker in 1902. Courtesy of the San Juan Capistrano Historical Society

in 1853. Her wedding, erroneously characterized as her first (mission records show otherwise), was described in *Capistrano Nights* using Polonia's own words and ended with:

"My great grandmother gave me this advice: "Polonia,' she said, 'if your husband says at midday it is midnight, you agree with him that it is midnight; and if at midnight he says it is midday, agree with him in that too.'" During the wedding the bridegroom's gift of gold coins was dropped by Polonia, a sign of bad luck. Polonia thought this might have been the cause of Francisco's early death. Yet they were married seventeen years before the sad occurrence, and ten years later in 1880, Polonia married her third husband, Dr. Isadore Simard, medical doctor and occultist, whom she outlived.

Polonia is remembered as the village midwife, but she was also the captain of the pueblo, meaning she had charge of the religious instruction of the village children during the years the mission was without a resident priest. Once, during an extreme drought, she decided that she and the children would pray for rain. The first day they marched to Dana Point, but had no success. The second day was the same, only this time they walked as far as Trabuco Canyon. On the third day they walked to Capistrano Beach and while they marched clouds began to gather. While at the beach it rained so hard that three wagons had to be dispatched to bring them home and no one ever again scoffed at Polonia's efforts. This story, which appears in *Capistrano Nights*, also appeared in Dr. Rowan's newspaper column

San Juan Elementary School resembled the depot in 1912.
It was the third school to be built on the site.
Courtesy of the San Juan Capistrano Historical Society

in 1890.

Today Polonia is remembered through the adobe which was her home. Still standing on Los Rios Street, the adobe has been restored and is featured on weekly walking tours conducted by the San Juan Capistrano Historical Society. In 1910, when Father O'Sullivan first met Polonia, a tiny chapel still existed on the north side of the front porch of her home. It was here that special services were held during the years when there was no priest in residence at the mission, particularly services involving the children. In 1974, an archaeological dig was conducted on the property and though several floors were found and bits of crockery and glass, nothing was discovered which could exactly pinpoint the date of construction. The team of students from California State University at Fullerton also analyzed pollens in the soil, but could draw no conclusions, though the adobe is believed to have been one of the forty constructed during 1794.

San Juan Capistrano was a peaceful, friendly community as the calendar approached 1920. Everyone knew everyone else and life was not overly tiring.

There had been the war, of course, with Capistrano sending fifteen of its sons to fight in

Europe. One of those who went was C. Russell Cook, who served in the Balloon Corps. Those who stayed at home, waiting for their sons to return, flew flags on their homes and waited patiently for letters to arrive. Mrs. Margaret Cook, who came to San Juan in 1915 to teach school, organized a Junior Red Cross during World War I. In 1919, some of the same girls joined the Camp Fire Girls, which she also started in town.

When the war ended and the boys were safely home, life in San Juan settled back into its quiet pattern. More and more cars were traveling through now that the main street was paved; farms were prosperous; marks of progress were everywhere — the school, electric light poles, the mission in its new dress.

"Part of the charm of the place is the atmosphere of content that pervades the valley," wrote a staff writer for *Harper's* magazine, who visited Capistrano around this time. "There is no straining after notoriety, no real estate agents, no land for sale, no subdivisions, but for all of that one must not conclude that the ruling spirits are not splendid, progressive men. There is good fellowship, a free from the heart hospitality among the people of the valley unique in itself, reminding visitors of the old days in California when the latch string was always and forever on the outside."

Father Humilus and a teacher, Will McPherson in 1907. The mission had no resident priest between 1886 and 1910. Courtesy of the San Juan Capistrano Historical Society

Here is a turn-of-century view of San Juan Capistrano, seen easterly across the valley. Courtesy of the San Juan Capistrano Historical Society

Montanez Adobe on Los Rios Street, built in 1794, is now owned by the city of San Juan Capistrano.
Courtesy of the San Juan Capistrano Historical Society

Here is the first street paved, done in 1915. The Vanderleck Home, now El Adobe Restaurant, is shown at left.
The view is of Camino Capistrano looking north.
Courtesy of the San Juan Capistrano Historical Society

San Juan Inn was rebuilt after a 1918 fire and was a popular eatery for many years,
across Camino Capistrano from the mission where the Trading Post today.
Courtesy of the First American Title Insurance Company

Chapter 6

Chasing Rainbows, Oranges, and the Past
1920 – 1940

"I'm Always Chasing Rainbows" was a hit song in the United States when the decade of the 1920s began and it would aptly characterize the decades to follow, for Americans diligently searched for that illusive pot of gold — in the 1920s out of pleasure and in the 1930s out of need.

The nation entered the decade on a wave of nationalism and prosperity which would grow to unequaled heights during the Coolidge administration. Yet these would not be the best years for farmers, saloon operators, and male chauvinists. The twenties was a decade of declining farm markets, Prohibition, and women's suffrage. It was also a time when the American public crept unaware into a social revolution which would bring the greatest changes since the Civil War.

The 1920s was a time of restlessness, characterized by a loss of values and intellectual disillusionment hidden under a facade of conservatism in politics and business. San Juan Capistrano experienced this duality, but the changes were subtle and longer in coming. The town was still in the midst of a growth period, and it still lay in the shadow of the mission.

Travelers passing through San Juan during the mid-twenties found themselves in a small town which resembled a miniature city. Many new buildings lined the streets including the imposing new Capistrano Hotel, completed in 1920 by Fred A. Stoffel. It was built south of the San Juan Inn, a restaurant which Fred and his wife, Louise, purchased in 1916, and had rebuilt in 1918 after the original burned down. A few more restaurants had opened; the Shamrock and Midway cafes were on the west side of the main thoroughfare and the Palms Cafe was on the east

side. There was also Congdon's Garage and the White Garage and a new store opened by Ferris Kelly and Carl Romer. The general store started in a building on the east side of the street, but was moved twice, first into the Oyharzabal building and later into a two-story that is today called the Provincial Building.

Business was thriving. More and more cars passed through the old mission town, many on their way to the new developments of Doheny Park (Capistrano Beach) and the Spanish Village-by-the-Sea (San Clemente). Many came specifically to see the mission which had grown in reputation and was now a must on everyone's California itinerary. A 1925 issue of *National Geographic* said:

"In recent years the mission has been restored as nearly as possible to its original state and it is now a shrine linking the present with the past, visited by hundreds of tourists every day as they travel over a new king's highway of concrete which passes a few yards from the mission gates and connects the two major cities of Southern California — Los Angeles and San Diego."

The planting done by Father O'Sullivan had grown and blossomed. A new wall, built with funds donated by the Edward L. Doheny family, replaced the old picket fence. But the greatest change was in Father Serra's chapel. In 1924, the mission was given an altar of carved, gilded cherry wood. It had come from Barcelona, Spain, although its workmanship hints of an original construction in Mexico, and had been sent to Los Angeles where it had been destined for a cathedral. Instead it was presented to Mission San Juan Capistrano for Father Serra's chapel arriving in 396 pieces and requiring

Hotel Capistrano, built in 1920, is seen here as it looked twenty years later.
It was located where Capistrano Plaza is today, near the intersection of
Camino Capistrano and Ortega Highway.
Courtesy of the First American Title Insurance Company

a year and a half to put together. The altar, which still stands in the chapel, is over three hundred years old. In 1933, it was given an antique value well over $100,000. Once the altar was installed and modifications were made to the chapel, services were once again held in the oldest church in California. Since 1891, they had been held in what is today the museum and gift shop wing of the mission because the Serra Chapel was considered unsafe.

Another attraction during the mid-twenties was the mission's famous pageant. "Nationwide interest attracted to the mission pageant of San Juan Capistrano, called the Epic Drama of California History, has resulted in Garnet Holme, author and director, being besieged with applications for outdoor plays," reported the *Register* in 1925. The story went on to say that Holme would soon present a play in Palm Springs and had been asked to do one in Yellowstone and Casa Grande, Arizona. Longtime residents recall that this pageant was performed during the summer on the mission grounds and was, for a time, very popular. When the play was abandoned, the mission pageant continued as a spectacle of music and the performance of traditional Mexican and Indian dances. In the 1940s, it was

switched from summer to St. Joseph's Day (March 19) and continues to this day. The pageant now includes children who perform the dances and features a procession and coronation of a king and queen.

Capistrano residents had no problem entertaining themselves. Saturday night was dance night with most of the dances being held in the old Woodmen's Hall. Dances were also held thirteen miles out of town at the San Juan Hot Springs and in neighboring communities, but the ones at home were the most well-attended because the musicians were local and knew everybody's favorite songs. For the more adventurous there was boxing in Congdon's Garage or participation in motorcycle races, the most famous being the Capistrano Hill Climb held until 1924 in Capistrano Beach. For a change of scene, one could hire Bill English's 1915 Ford and go to Santa Ana or the beach, or one could ride horses over the hills or onto the beach.

One of the most popular forms of entertainment was movies. Until he built his slick new movie theater on the north side of the Capistrano Hotel (where the Trading Post is today), Fred Cason showed movies in the old Woodmen's Hall. His power source was unique. He would park his Model T Ford outside, jack up the rear wheel and put a belt on it, running the belt into the building where his projector was.

"Sometimes kids would come along and pull out the choke," said Reggie Nieblas. "Then Mr. Cason would have to come outside and start up the car again."

Pranksters had no trouble amusing themselves in the San Juan of the 1920s. On another occasion a full-grown cow was led up the stairs of the posh Capistrano Hotel during the night. The jokesters then fled, leaving the animal bellowing in the second-floor corridor while frightened guests peered cautiously out of their doors, then frantically called out for the dozing night clerk. The same gang put a goat in Judge John Landell's office in downtown San Juan. During the night the goat got hungry and when the judge opened the door the next morning, he found bits of tattered paper littering his desk, where the morning's cases should have been.

Town youngsters didn't just play tricks on judges and hotelkeepers. They also had fun at the expense of local bootleggers. The twenties was a decade of Prohibition, but like most other towns, San Juan always had a ready supply. Saloons were closed, but no wedding or wake was complete without its moonshine. If you were careful, it was relatively easy to make your own brew. Carl Stroschein, later town constable, tried making his own beer in the cellar of his house (the home of the Chamber of Commerce in 1990). One night it blew up, so he gave up the idea.

Whatever one's feelings toward Prohibition, bootlegging was still against the law and many believed in temperance. The editor of the town's only local newspaper, the weekly *Coastline Dispatch*, had this to say about the community's Fourth of July celebration in 1931:

"San Juan Capistrano is congratulating itself that the recent marathon celebration on July 4 was marked by an absence of any disorderly conduct, and that no drinking or carousing marred the day, which is as it should be and the committee in charge deserves much credit. But just the same this human scribe can't help wondering if the theft of 21 gallons of booze from the home of Capistrano's leading bootlegger, a few days before the fourth, had anything to do with the absence of liquor at the celebration. Now don't ask us who Capistrano's leading bootleggers are for we don't know; all we know is that the theft was not reported to the sheriff and that some other community probably got what was made for local consumption."

Fred Stoffel, standing, greets guests at the San Juan Inn in the 1920s. He later built the Capistrano Hotel.
Courtesy of Fred Stoffel

The first San Juan Inn, which may have occupied the original depot building, burned down in 1918.
Courtesy of the San Juan Capistrano Historical Society

Rum-running wasn't the only crime to plague local law enforcement officials. There was also the usual number of thefts, vagrants, and reckless drivers. The smuggling of Chinese into California was a common practice (exclusion acts specifically barred them at this time), and many passed through Capistrano on their way from Mexico to San Francisco. But the most unusual crime of the twenties to take place in San Juan was a robbery and murder which happened on a speeding train. It was the last train robbery to take place in Orange County, according to historian Jim Sleeper.

"One hundred officers Hunt Mail Robber" was the banner headline in the *Santa Ana Register* August 25, 1925. The story told how a daring assailant had robbed the mail car, shot the attendant, and escaped leaving no clues for officials in two counties — Los Angeles and Orange — to follow.

"Mail and mail pouches and an overturned and rifled strongbox on the floor of the car, together with the body of the wounded man, told a mute story when railroad employees opened the door at 8:42

p.m. as the flyer pulled into the Santa Ana station," the story said.

It was speculated that the crime — the assailant on the roof of the railroad car, kicking in the glass, shooting down into the car — happened while the train was on a dead run through the Capistrano area. The train wasn't scheduled to stop and didn't even slow down as it traveled through town.

After killing the attendant, the criminal lowered himself over the side of the speeding train using a rope ladder with large hooks on top which he anchored to the roof. He then broke the glass window of the door, reached through the jagged opening to unfasten the latch, collected his loot, and escaped. Officials theorized that he either jumped from the train as it slowed to enter Santa Ana and left on foot, or he had an accomplice with a car waiting. Another theory was that he leaped from the speeding train somewhere outside of Capistrano so he could catch the southbound as it passed.

On August 26, the *Register* reported that only five dollars had been in the rifled strongbox. But a

Here is a view of downtown looking north about 1925.
Courtesy of the First American Title Insurance Company

story three days later revealed that $2,100 had been taken from the mail sacks. Reward posters were circulated and police followed numerous leads, but the criminal was never found. By then the charge was murder, for Elmer Campbell, a 32-year employee of Santa Fe who had been in the posses that had tracked Jesse James and Geronimo, had died.

Crimes were big news in the Capistrano Valley. In 1923, people could read about them in their own hometown newspaper, *The Missionite*. Started as a high school paper, it became a professional publication by Frank Winterbourne. When E. B. and M. A. Dupree took it over (around 1930) the name was changed to

Coastline Dispatch. Later publishers were Cy Summers, in the late 1930s, Neal Weatherholt from 1941 to 1955, Robert Hancock and Larry Hernandez from 1955 to 1961. In 1990, the paper was published by Stanford Manning and is no longer

Tito Goodwins house, now location of The Swallows Inn.
Courtesy of the San Juan Capistrano Historical Society

White Garage on Camino Capistrano was located where the main entrance to Antiques Barn is today.
Courtesy of the First American Title Insurance Company

printed in San Juan Capistrano. Thanks to Hernandez, old issues of the Dispatch were collected and bound and still exist at the offices of the Sun-Post in San Clemente.

Elections were of even greater interest, especially those involving schools. In 1919, Capistrano Union High School District was founded, serving the San Juan Capistrano and Serra Grammar School districts. The first trustees were C. E. Crumrine, J. S. Landell, Guy Williams, C. Russell Cook, and Mae Forster. Sixteen students were housed in a temporary building which opened September 13, 1920, with John S. Malcom, principal, and one teacher. The curriculum included English, Latin I, mathematics, Spanish, history and athletics. Residents of the Capistrano Valley no longer had to send their children to Santa Ana. The permanent school opened in 1921 on a ten acre site between Highway 101 (Camino Capistrano) and El Camino Real with classrooms, a shop, and a 400-seat auditorium. The first graduates, in 1923, were Lucana Forster Isch and Marian Barnes, who had previously attended school in Santa Ana. Another early graduate was Dr. Herbert Stroschein who, along with others imbued with school spirit, carried wooden planks up the highest hill opposite the school in 1921 and built the "C" which still stands. In 1923, it was lowered by twenty feet for better visibility. The emblem was converted to

concrete in the early 1930s, to protect it from the hooves of wandering cattle, and from then on was the site of numerous rituals of cleaning and painting for incoming freshmen.

A lively interest in politics was typical of rural communities in America and San Juan was still very much a small town. Despite its prosperous downtown business district and its tourist-filled mission, most of the area was still comprised of large farms. The major crop was still walnuts, planted in the valleys. Wheat and barley were harvested on the hillsides and cattle still roamed the vast expanses east of the town. Truck crops, primarily beans and tomatoes, were planted in the lowlands, and a new crop was beginning to dominate the northern valleys — oranges. In 1913, the Williams families purchased land from Judge Richard Egan near the confluence of the Oso and Trabuco Creek. Brothers R. Y. and Guy Williams along with Mrs. Guy Williams' own brothers, Will and Sim Bathgate, were doing well when Louis DeJean of *Overland Monthly* interviewed them in 1929.

"Six times the average yield is the proud record of Guy Williams' orange groves this year and Judge R. Y. Williams has for years been transferring bean fields and waste stretches of this valley into walnuts and citrus," wrote DeJean. He noted that the Bathgates were shipping fat green tomatoes to the Eastern markets and had

People park in front of Palm Cafe on the east side of Camino Capistrano, converted from the old schoolhouse in 1912.
Courtesy of the First American Title Insurance Company

many other crops planted as well.

The Williams' are generally credited with starting the citrus industry in Capistrano which grew into its major business in the thirties and forties. Although earlier settlers had experimented with orange-growing, most of their groves had disappeared when the Williams family planted theirs. During the 1920s, many of the town's residents helped with the orange harvest. Major employers were still farms and ranches, though the work was somewhat seasonal and sometimes required travel to other nearby communities.

Agriculture remained the mainstay of San Juan's economy when the nation entered the Great Depression. It provided employment and food for some, yet for others there was no work, no money, and nothing to eat. One resident recalled subsisting on a diet of fish, cabbage, and whatever he could trap in the nearby Cleveland National Forest. Another remembered eating dried apricots until she couldn't stand the sight of them. Some confessed to poaching on the O'Neill Ranch. The Works Progress Administration put some people to work building roads and firebreaks, and a Civilian Conservation Corps opened in the nearby national forest, though most of its workers were imported

Unroofed corridors of the mission's north wing were reconstructed by Father O'Sullivan. The school is in the background.
Courtesy of Alfonso Yorba

Mission restoration and reconstruction was done under the leadership of Father O'Sullivan.
Courtesy of Alfonso Yorba

gold nuggets supposedly found during these long-ago expeditions. The story created a flurry of interest in San Juan. Some residents came forward to dispute the claims, while others swore that the mine existed. One man who had operated a mine in Lucas Canyon was Henry Stewart, Sr., whose claim was supposedly jumped in 1922. It was rumored that his wife, Mrs. Ruth Stewart, could verify his success as she had several nuggets in a safe deposit box in Santa Ana. No further reports were made on the progress of the mine and enthusiasm quietly died.

But rainbow chasing didn't. On February 10, 1933, the *Coastline Dispatch* reported that a test was being made on a wildcat oil well two miles east of San Juan Capistrano. "Geologists believe an oil field is imminent," readers learned. Tests continued to be made in the well, located on the Cornelio

from another state. The town was loaded with vagrants, many of them knocking on back doors looking for something to eat. Stomachs were empty and work was scarce. It was time to look for the pot of gold at the end of a rainbow.

"A search is underway for the Lost Mine of the Padres," read Capistrano residents when they opened their weekly *Coastline Dispatch* on August 28, 1931. "Leases held by O. K. Carr of Santa Ana promise to yield rewards that will dwarf all other California gold claims."

The story continued that for the past 150 years a "certain area" fifteen miles northeast of town had been known by old Spanish residents as one rich in gold nuggets. Oldtimers recalled hearing stories about the padres sending hundreds of Indians to find the gold hidden in the canyons. No records were kept stating how much gold had been found. But some longtime residents could produce

Workmen hand-made adobe bricks to build the wall around the front of the mission in the mid-1920s.
Courtesy of Alfonso Yorba

Echenique ranch. The oil field, which was soon discovered, would be developed by the Mineral Exploration Company. Another test was being made in the Trabuco area of the O'Neill Ranch.

The oil tests ran into problems. Water continually flowed into the well and had to be drained. Yet the quality of the oil was high and promoters felt sure that enough would be discovered for commercial production. A large area of the Echenique Ranch was leased. A big strike was expected daily. Capistrano

A mission wall was constructed in the mid-1920s with funds donated by the E.L. Doheny family.
Courtesy of the First American Title Insurance Company

residents, with dollar signs in their eyes, started talking about incorporation. The oil strike, like the Lost Mine of the Padres, failed to materialize and the pot of gold faded away. People shook their heads, chided themselves about being dreamers, and vowed never again to believe. Until the next time.

The next time came in 1935.

"If preliminary surveys of the property are any indication, the Old Dominion may equal or surpass the famed Silver Queen at Mojave, California's most famous property." Those were the words of Norris H. Hilton, a mining authority, who opened the Old Dominion Mine twenty-six miles northeast of San Juan Capistrano. Already over one million dollars in ore has been blocked out by surveyors of the property, he added. "Ore so valuable that gold and silver-bearing rocks assayed at $91 per ton will be merely a by product," stated the Santa Ana man.

The mine was first opened in 1885 by Jim Balfour of Elsinore, who worked it until a railroad company obtained a patent to the land and forced him out. The mine contained its own smelter and apricot pits were used for fuel. The ore was taken in wagons to Elsinore and shipped to Oakland. It was last worked in 1896. But the mine was said to need a

Graves were relocated to Mission Cemetery when Serra Chapel was enlarged.
Courtesy of the San Juan Capistrano Historical Society

Serra Chapel was remodeled and enlarged in the 1920s to accommodate a gilded cherry-wood altar.
Courtesy of Alfonso Yorba

purposes of growing eggplant, lettuce, sweet potatoes, and bell peppers. The following October the company announced it would lease and repair the old grain storage house on the corner of McKinley and the railroad tracks (southeast corner of Verdugo and tracks where the parking structure is today) and would soon be hiring forty to sixty people to pack tomatoes, celery, and cauliflower. Other signs of recovery were evident. A new Ford and a new Chevrolet dealership opened downtown, though

"highly specialized process" in order to refine the ore. And, like all the others, this dream died.

Some residents continued to poke around the hills, looking for gold. Some found it and brought it into town to be traded for supplies. Nuggets whose rough edges tantalized the finder who knew they couldn't have been in the stream bed long, were often brought into town to be weighed on Carl Romer's gold scale. But the main vein continued to elude the prospectors. Even Maximo Lopez, who was said to always have a nugget or two, never found the mother lode. A few caught the silver fever when in 1939 a silver strike was supposedly discovered in Modjeska Canyon. Rumors flew. A million and a half dollars worth would be offered for claim. A few ventured on the dream, but most did not.

The town's economy had suffered a major setback when the First State Bank closed in 1932. The bank, which had opened its doors to a prosperous town eight years earlier, failed because of a lack of depositors, according to bank officials quoted in the newspaper. Assets were auctioned for fifty-one dollars and one note, collected on by its new owner, turned out to be worth five hundred dollars.

A favorable sign appeared in January 1932, when a company called the American Fruit Growers leased seven hundred acres of the Santa Margarita, Echenique, and Forster ranches for the

A gilded cherry-wood altar designed for a cathedral was instead reassembled in Serra Chapel.
Courtesy of the San Juan Capistrano Historical Society

106

Dancers in the mission pageant were all local people. In the foreground are Nieves and Fidel Sepulveda. Others in the pageant cast included Doc Belardes, Delfina Olivares, Filomena Ricardes, Andres Garcia, Felipe Garcia, Bessie Ruiz, George Avila, Reyes Yorba, Lula Avila, Bill Jimenez, and Ramon Yorba.
Courtesy of the San Juan Capistrano Historical Society

to purchase the land on which the packing house stood, and a bit of land around it for future expansion. In 1932 alone, San Juan's orange crop had been 148,000 boxes. Oranges had become one of the town's leading industries and was growing fast. Walnuts had not yet disappeared, nor would they until after World War II. Truck crops were still productive and cattle still roamed the outlying ranch districts. People began to have a little change in their pockets and could now turn their attention to other things. They could park downtown on a Sunday afternoon and watch the tourists who continued to visit San Juan, despite the Depression, and they could think about what it must have been like in the old days.

The 1930s brought a reawakened interest in the history of San Juan Capistrano. The newspaper was filled with articles, many of them written by local historian Alfonso Yorba, detailing what was then known about the various adobes and the town's historic sites. Fund drives were launched

most people recall that these businesses were more garages than showrooms. Tony Nydegger and C. Russell Cook took steps to get men interested in forming a new volunteer fire department. Carl Hankey was named chairman of a committee to organize the first Chamber of Commerce; a contract was let to G. K. Sanborn to build the Ortega Highway between San Juan Capistrano and the Hot Springs. When complete, the Ortega would be paved all the way to Elsinore.

In 1933, the American Fruit Growers opened its packing house in San Juan Capistrano, equipped mainly to process oranges. The fruit, which would be marketed under the Blue Goose label, would be processed by local labor in the newly renovated building next to the railroad tracks. It would no longer be necessary for farmers to have their citrus hauled to Orange or other northern county locations for processing and marketing. A year later the company negotiated with Frank and John Forster and with Esteban Oyharzabal

Musicians played for all the local dances. Many were held in the Woodmen's Hall, a converted Protestant church.
Courtesy of the San Juan Capistrano Historical Society

The Capistrano Hill Climb was a popular motorcycle race until 1924 when the event ended. It was held south of town near Capistrano Beach.
Courtesy of the San Juan Capistrano Historical Society

are thousands of better business towns, thousands of more progressive people, thousands of more modern places in which to live; stripped of its historical interest and value, San Juan Capistrano is but a wide place in the road."

Businesses depend on tourists, he added. Without the mission and its lore, the tourists wouldn't stop: "Let us not forget the more of these traditions we can preserve and revive, the more interest we will have for the world at large."

People listened and responded. For the first time since Spanish had been the major language cafes began to bear Spanish names. Streets that had been Anglicized were changed thanks to a drive spearheaded by local historian Alfonso Yorba; McKinley became Del Obispo, Garden became Verdugo, and Oriental Street returned to El Camino Real. Occidental Street became Los Rios Street and Central was changed to Camino Capistrano. Most of the new names had historical significance. The town began to capitalize on its heritage — the mission's influence had inadvertently taken a new turn.

One offshoot of the trend was an interest in historic preservation outside the mission walls. In 1937, an adobe located between the Canedo Adobe and the former Miguel Verdugo house (and attached by a common wall to both), on the east side of El Camino Real south of Ortega Highway, was taken down brick by brick. The house contained eight hundred whole and four hundred half bricks, four shutters, five hand-hewn beams, one double and single door, and five corridor posts. The structure, built in 1852 by Tomas Ramos, an ancestor of the Ramos family which still resides in San Juan, changed hands several times before becoming a cantina, billiard parlor, and dance hall of Miguel Yorba at the end of the last century. It was then called Casa de Azul because of its blue exterior color. In taking the building down it was discovered that the wall that had joined the building to the Verdugo adobe on the south side was made of materials common to the 1794 construction of Indian adobes. The entire set of building materials was purchased and stored by Alfonso Yorba for future restoration, but no one knows where.

A drive was also launched to save the nearby Casa Tejada, another building believed to have been of 1794 construction. The "house of tile" was used

to help with the mission's restoration. Contributors included many people untouched by the Depression. One was William Randolph Hearst. Renewed interest in history caused the formation of the Spanish California Club. In June, the town held a Mexican fiesta and parade. Businessmen were encouraged to wear Spanish dress during this fiesta and during the San Diego Exposition of 1934, which drew many travelers who passed through San Juan. *The Coastline's* editor encouraged people to take pride in their heritage, pointing out that the past is what made the town unique, and gave it a financial advantage:

"There is little or no interest to be attached to San Juan Capistrano from a modern point of view. The only thing that makes the place of interest to the outside world is the history surrounding it. There

by mayordomos of the mission. Blas Aguilar bought it in 1841 from Zeferino Taroge, the last Indian chanter of the mission, according to Alfonso Yorba. The north wing of the building was called Casa de Esperanza and was successfully restored by Juan Aguilar, grandson of Blas. In it he placed antiques from early California and many family treasures, hoping to make it a museum. But he died in November of 1936. The Casa de Esperanza (now called the Blas Aguilar Adobe) still stands today next to the old Pacific Telephone building on El Camino Real, and it is now a museum. The Casa Tejada, however, was destroyed.

Like the Casa Tejada, other buildings could not be saved. The famous Mendelson Mission Inn, a large wooden structure between the Casa Tejada and the Burruel adobes on El Camino Real was torn down. It had stood since 1875, according to Richard Mendelson, whose grandparents bought the hotel site and some land behind it in 1874. In 1933, the building was considered a fire trap and was razed a few years later. Auxiliary buildings, attached to the hotel, stood behind the Burruel adobe ruins until they were removed in 1975.

Fire was a very real problem until the volunteer fire department was formed in the early 1930s. Before the volunteers were organized, Tony Nydegger kept an old fire engine in a garage where Cedar Creek is today and was a one-man fire company. Once a person called him on the phone and said "Tony, come quickly, my barn is on fire." Unfortunately the person failed to leave his name, but because it was a small town, Tony recognized the voice, and knew where to go.

The thirties were not just a time for destruction of the buildings that had not withstood the wear and tear of time, it was also a time for building. In 1936, when the San Juan Hot Springs closed, all of its buildings were offered for sale and most of them were moved to Capistrano. Twenty-seven cabins were placed on Mission Flats, a former swamp south of Mission Hill. The street names in this subdivision designated former use of the land during the mission period — La Matanza (the slaughterhouse), La Calera (the limekiln), El Homo (the oven, used for tilemaking) and Acjachema (a derivative of the word Acagcheme, a local Indian name). Many of the little hot springs houses were renovated; some were torn down. A few still stand

in the tract today.

Building activity also took place on the hill above. A former pasture, the area had also been subdivided along with Mission Flats in 1926 with twenty-one lots being sold the first week. Among early residents were Dr. and Mrs. Paul Esslinger whose home was a showplace of Capistrano as early as 1933. Although plastered inside and out, the house was built in the tradition of old Capistrano, using adobe bricks. The house still stands and in 1990 was the home of the Maurice Fetterman family.

The construction of homes in the Capistrano Valley offered visitors who liked the area a chance to stay, and many did. The town they found was small and friendly and had strong community identity. The mission was still the focal point of the town, but the schools were the social centers. Every football game, every talent show, and school play had capacity audiences. School board meetings were well-attended and school board actions were discussed in every barbershop and drawing room.

Judge John Landell was Justice of the Peace for San Juan Capistrano for many years.
Courtesy of Gladys Landell Garrity

Bootleggers operated off the coast of Dana Point, and were frequently captured.
Courtesy of the First American Title Insurance Company

said yes. When the election was over, there were some who whispered that the board had wanted the $45,000 all along, but knew better than to ask for it the first time. The new wing was built and completed in 1939.

The year 1938 was not only the year bonds were passed for school expansion. It was also the year of the big flood. In March, the town was inundated with days of rain and every auto and railroad bridge washed out, isolating the town. Men had to be posted at crossings with lanterns during the night to warn the unwary. No one could get in or out of San Juan Capistrano. Despite precautions, there was tragedy. Sim Bathgate and C. W. Parks, attempting to save a water line, were swept into the angry river. Parks' body was recovered downstream, but Bathgate's was never found.

The town recovered from the effects of the disastrous flood; bridges were rebuilt and life went

Supporting the activities of one's children didn't always mean supporting the actions of the Board of Trustees.

In April of 1938, the Capistrano Union High School District Board of Trustees decided the high school should be expanded to accommodate the town's spurt of growth. They asked the voters to approve a $160,000 bond issue, and the fight was on. The election was held in May and bitter words flew from both sides. When the votes were counted, the nays won. But that didn't stop the school board. It passed another resolution, this time asking for a $65,000 bond issue. The election was held in July with more bitter words and the bonds, again, lost. Undaunted, the board came right back and at the end of the month asked the voters to approve a $45,000 bond issue. The election was held in August and people in San Juan, San Clemente, Dana Point, and Capistrano Beach

Capistrano Union High School opened in 1921. The building is now gone.
Courtesy of the San Juan Capistrano Historical Society

In this aerial view looking north in 1929, the mission is at center.
Courtesy of Alfonso Yorba

on. People picked up their newspapers and again read about the progress of the high school athletic teams, always featured on the front page, or the latest blue ribbon awarded to Carl Hankey's gladiolus. Some turned the page to check the activities of the Woman's Club, Rotary, Woman's Auxiliary of the Mission, and Sportsman's Club. Many service clubs got their start in the 1930s although some, like the Woman's Club, were already flourishing in the twenties. People could also read about something unique to San Juan Capistrano, something that had been present all along, yet had gone unnoticed. It took outsiders to discover what would be labeled the mystique of San Juan Capistrano, what would give the town distinction among all other small towns of the United States — its swallows.

For years bird lovers had visited the mission ruins to study the nesting habits of the swallow. In 1915, long before the legend of the swallows' punctual return was publicized, a writer in *Overland Monthly* remarked how the swallows liked to nest in the mission and told the story of Pepita Arrequa,

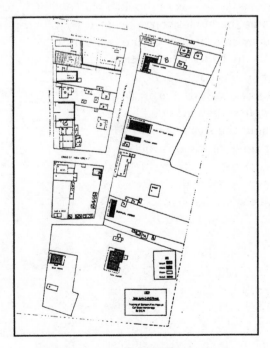

This Sanborn map of 1929 shows the location of structures in downtown.
Courtesy of the City of San Juan Capistrano

*The Tower Building was originally a gas station in the 1920s.
It was located in El Camino Real Park near Oso Road.
Later it served as a residence. It was torn
down in early 1970s.*

about patching up their broken nests, building new ones and disputing possession of others with such vagrant sparrow families as may have taken up illegal quarters there during the swallows' absence. On this fragment of broken adobe walls ... you will see them pecking the soil and with a great flutter of wings carrying it off as building material. They fly with it to the old mission laguna (pond) off there to the northeast of the buildings, and with water make a paste of the earth in their little beaks, amid more fluttering of wings at the pond's edge. Then a straight course to the mission's eaves to deliver their loads of mud plaster for the walls of their inverted houses, and receive the noisy congratulations of their mates."

who believed in the mission's eventual restoration, though weeds were shoulder high and only swallows came there. Her son, a talented sculptor, eventually returned to help with the restoration.

In 1930, when Father O'Sullivan and Charles Saunders put together the book called *Capistrano Nights*, they included a story about the swallows. A padre, angered at the destruction of swallows' nests by a hotel-keeper, opened his arms and welcomed the birds to the mission. They nested there ever since.

"By the way there is a very odd fact about these swallows," said Father O'Sullivan. "You know, they migrate every autumn, but their return is with the greatest regularity on Saint Joseph's Day, the nineteenth of March. Within a few days they set

This account was the first time the legend of the swallows had been published nationally. The story was colorful and quaint, but nobody in Chicago

*This handball court was located behind what is today the Provincial Building.
Courtesy of the San Juan Capistrano Historical Society*

112

Las Rosas, the home of Marcos Forster, built in 1882, was a hotel for a short time before becoming a restaurant in the 1930s.
Courtesy of the First American Title Insurance Company

rushed to buy a ticket to Capistrano to see the swallows return. Not yet. Not until Ed Ainsworth began to publicize them in his newspaper column.

Ed Ainsworth, state editor of the *Los Angeles Times*, was fond of the mission. The legend of the swallows intrigued him, so on March 19 he would always note in his column that the swallows had returned, on schedule, to Capistrano. He had never been present for the return, but a quick phone call to the mission would confirm the presence of the birds and he'd write his column in good faith. In 1936, an unexpected event took place. A famous broadcaster called and told Ainsworth he had decided to broadcast to the world the return of the swallows. According to Mrs. Ainsworth, her husband was panic-stricken. He hurriedly made a trip to the mission to check with his friend Father Arthur J. Hutchinson to be sure the birds would arrive on time that year. The good father could not give any guarantees, but he could pray. They both could pray. On the morning of March 19, the broadcasting equipment was set up on the mission grounds and two thousand people watched the skies. One of the visitors was Gov. Frank Merriman. Ainsworth

Carl Stroschein and Alfonso Yorba converse in the mission. Carl was constable of San Juan Township and Alfonso was the local historian.
Courtesy of Ruth Stroschein

consulted his watch. No swallows. Father Hutchinson looked worried. People laughed nervously and fidgeted as the day went on. Some roamed the town, while others took up their vigil in restaurants and bars; several gave up and went home. Then, just as Ainsworth was about to lose hope, a shout went up and the largest flock of swallows ever to descend on the mission flew in. The broadcaster reported to the world that the "skies were blackened with swallows" and the legend was safely launched. From then on the swallows were front page news in the *Coastline Dispatch*, which strangely had never before noted their presence. They were also front page news in such distant places as Chicago, New York, and Miami.

The swallows would have more impact on San Juan Capistrano than any other single event in the twentieth century. Although longtime residents recalled rising at dawn to sit with Father O'Sullivan in front of the mission, awaiting the return of the swallows on St. Joseph's Day, others in the community had paid little attention to the return of the noisy birds until the year of the first broadcast. Announcing the return became an annual event. On March 19, 1959, a songwriter named Leon Rene sat waiting for his breakfast. Hearing that the swallows were due he turned to his wife and said he probably would have to wait until the swallows came

back to Capistrano for his breakfast. The thought gave him the idea for the song, "When The Swallows Come Back to Capistrano," which was recorded by twelve nationally known artists. Recordings sold over three million copies.

Ironically the man who first wrote down the legend of the swallows was not present to see it grow to national proportions. Father St. John O'Sullivan, who was invested as Monsignor in his hospital bed, died in July of 1933. Although first buried elsewhere, he was finally laid to rest in the garden of his beloved mission.

By the end of the thirties, San Juan Capistrano was a town that people all over the United States had heard of. Not only did it have its "jewel of the missions" it also had its swallows. The decade had begun disastrously, but was not without its accomplishments — completion of the Ortega Highway, the enlargement of the high school, the reawakening of interest in cultural heritage, and the promotion of the swallows. The future looked promising; people could laugh about those rainbow-chasing days. They were on a solid foundation again.

Palm Cafe stood at the corner of Yorba and Camino Capistrano.
Courtesy of the San Juan Capistrano Historical Society

Eulalia Soto and Lula Avila dressed as mission tour guides in 1932.
Courtesy of the San Juan Capistrano Historical Society

This garage in the center was located where Cedar Creek Restaurant is today.
It once housed the first volunteer fire department truck, owned by Tony Nydegger.
Courtesy of the First American Title Insurance Company

Blas Aguilar Adobe (Casa Esperanza) is shown with Casa Tejada now gone.
Courtesy of Alfonso Yorba

The flood of 1938 was as serious as the flood of 1916, seen here in view of the
washed-out Santa Fe bridge over San Juan creek looking east.
Courtesy of the San Juan Capistrano Historical Society

Rouse Cottage was built in the 1880s on the Hot Springs Road, now Ortega Highway.
Courtesy of the San Juan Capistrano Historical Society

Rouse Cottage was occupied for many years by Carl and Adele Hankey,
who grew oranges on the property.
Courtesy of the San Juan Capistrano Historical Society

8 Mile Marathon winners, San Juan Capistrano, July 4, 1929. Charles Belardes #1 - $25, 51 min., 15 sec., John Manriquez #216 - $15.00, Paul Lobo #21 - $10.00, Joe Yorba #10 - $6.00, Bill Rosenbaum #6 - $5.00.
Courtesy of the San Juan Capistrano Historical Society

Father O'Sullivan's funeral service was held in the Great Stone Church ruins on November 7, 1934. He was first buried in Los Angeles on July 22, 1933, and later re-buried in his beloved mission.
Courtesy of the San Juan Capistrano Historical Society

These men are seen here surveying the route of the Ortega Highway in 1932.
Courtesy of the San Juan Capistrano Historical Society

Ortega Highway planners in 1930, from left, were George Jeffrey, Ferris Kelly, Carl Hankey, Frank Champion,
William Griswold, and Willard Smith
Courtesy of the San Juan Capistrano Historical Society

Swallows gather mud for their nests. Known as "cliff swallows," the birds return to the old mission every March 19.
Courtesy of Duane Hallan

Swallows build nests of tiny granules of mud and attach them to eaves. They are said to return each year to the same nest.
Courtesy of Duane Hallan

Shown here are Acu Jose de Garcia Cruz and his friend Jose Juan Olivares. Acu first recounted the story of the swallows in Capistrano Nights, *a book published in 1930. Courtesy of the San Juan Capistrano Historical Society*

Magdalena Murillo, a character in Capistrano Nights, *lived in Avila Adobe, which was partially rebuilt after the fire. Courtesy of the San Juan Capistrano Historical Society*

Tom and Alice Forster, children of Frank and Ada Forster, are seen here in front of Casa Grande.
Courtesy of the San Juan Capistrano Historical Society

This is a view of Camino Capistrano looking north in 1931. Richfield station, at right, is where the mini park is today.
Courtesy of the San Juan Capistrano Historical Society

Chapter 7

Inklings of War
1940 – 1960

In the twenties and thirties, Americans wrapped themselves snugly in a cocoon of isolationism and focused all their attention on a domestic metamorphosis. But by 1939, they could no longer ignore increasing tensions of the world situation. Though attempting neutrality, the country was violently thrust into World War II on December 7, 1941. The cocoon opened and a stronger United States took its place as a world power.

The war years brought a new sense of community to the American public. People who had been nodding acquaintances before now gathered to receive instruction in first aid and raise funds for the Red Cross. Fourth of July picnics enjoyed a revival; flag manufacturers grew prosperous, and everyone waited anxiously for the arrival of the mail. San Juan also had its sons, nephews, and husbands fighting overseas. The town, which always had a strong community identity, grew closer. Neighbors gathered in each other's homes to learn civil defense and the planting of victory gardens. Exceeding the quota on scrap metal drives was a matter of civic pride.

While still the geographic center of the town, focus grew away from the mission during the 1940s. War-related activities consumed everyone's attention, and when the war ended, the focus was on the town itself and a new issue, growth. The growth issue of the forties and fifties was not how big the town would grow, but would it grow at all, and the answer to this question would directly influence two of the most important issues of the 1960s — the importation of water and the location of the new high school. But as people hung up their 1940 calendars these issues

were still far away — as far away as the war that was beginning to take shape in Europe. War news, what little there was, appeared on the back pages of the local newspaper. School activities, sports events, and club meetings still dominated the front page: the swallows left early; the play, entitled *Miracle of the Swallows* might be revived; a parent protest was underway to get the schools back to the three 'Rs.

In September, the war abroad was brought home briefly when teachers at Capistrano Union High School swore an oath of allegiance denouncing "all fifth column activities and all subversive activities." The action made state headlines and national news. One month later the local draft board, which acted mostly on agricultural deferrals, was set up. Its members were Les Remmers, John Keresy, Clarence Brown, Dr. Paul Esslinger, and Maj. J. W. Woolridge. But the war was still far away. It hadn't yet intruded on the peace of San Juan Capistrano. The feeling of isolation continued through 1941. A home guard was organized, just as a precaution. Sponsored by the Sportsman's Club, the group held drills and counted fifty men from Capistrano, Dana Point, and Doheny Park among its rank. Many locals joined the armed forces right after graduation, since jobs were still hard to find. But the United States was still officially neutral, and though everyone had his own opinion on who was right and who was wrong, most expected the war to remain a distant occurrence, something that was happening to someone else.

An occasional newcomer drifted into town,

The Mendelson Family raised chicken and turkeys behind their hotel on El Camino Real.
Courtesy of the San Juan Capistrano Historical Society

conditions were good at home. The local orange packing house doubled its production and had seventy-five people on its payroll. Walnut growers were having a good year. Land still occasionally changed hands, such as the 5,000-acre ranch purchased by oil magnate E. G. Starr northeast of town. People had plenty to talk about when they turned on their radios on a lazy Sunday morning to hear the news that would dominate conversations all over the United States. Like people in other towns, the news of December 7, 1941, caught them off guard.

"Japan Attacks the American Island Possession in the Pacific Sunday," read

some quietly, others with a little more flamboyance. One who attracted plenty of attention was Harry Oliver. Harry was not an ordinary businessman. A former Hollywood art director, he had such films as the *Good Earth* and *Viva Villa* to his credit. He also claimed to have been assistant art director for *Ben Hur* and designer of the famous Van de Kamp windmills. Harry set up his Old Mission Trading Post next to Tony's Garage on the corner of El Camino Real and Ortega Highway. He had a wide selection of western relics and a couple of dozen copies of his book, *Desert Rough Cuts*. Harry had a couple of other things in his back room, according to historian Jim Sleeper. Fond of the desert and its folklore, Harry greatly enjoyed carving wooden legs which he used in his own form of leg-pulling. On his many trips into the desert he would scatter them around and would then read with interest about the latest discovery of the lost peg-leg mine.

Harry Oliver injected a bit of humor into a town that was beginning to worry about the worsening situation in Europe. Yet economic

the banner headline in the *Coastline Dispatch* the following week. Capistrano had also experienced its first blackout alarm, but not everyone had cooperated. The idea was too new; the necessity still alien.

By December 19, a civilian defense council was organized. An observation tower was quickly constructed, fashioned from the old water tower that stood on Mission Hill at the end of Andres Pico Street, and a call went out for volunteers to act as sky scanners. Classes were organized to instruct people in first aid, conduct during blackouts, and how to disarm bombs. An official home militia was formed, part of the statewide unit. And in July of 1942, San Juan residents read about the U.S. Navy's acquisition of the 133,000-acre Santa Margarita Ranch to be used as a Marine Corps center. It was to be called Camp Pendleton. The war was suddenly very close.

Rationing brought the war into every home in San Juan Capistrano. It began with sugar and spread quickly to other products. Luxury items were particularly scarce. When a new shipment of nylon stockings arrived at the local department store, downtown businesses with female employees closed early so women could get in line. The lines sometimes stretched for two blocks.

But the casualty lists brought the war even closer. The first San Juan boy killed in action was Malcolm L. Conner. The next was Aciano Avila. The losses were not confined to single families, they were shared by the entire town. San Juan was like that. A person's grief was his neighbors'. Yet life went on. There was work to be done, crops to be planted and harvested, workers to be housed, volunteers to round up for the local USO, and lists to be checked for the "eyes aloft" program.

The scanning program had no lack of volunteers. Old-timers, teenagers, housewives, businessmen — everyone took a turn sitting in the tower watching for planes. But finding workers for the farms was more difficult. Most men were in the

service. Some were called to work in nearby towns in war-related manufacturing concerns, and had to turn their town businesses over to their high school-age children. T. J. Meadows took over his father's ice business before entering the Navy when his father was called to work in Long Beach. The ice house, which is today part of Durenberger's Antiques, still stands on Camino Capistrano. High school students were also asked to help with the harvest. Those who came from out of town were housed in the high school. The orange crop was a large one in 1942, though it was not a good year for walnuts. Devastated by pests like the husk fly and coddling moth worm, walnuts had all but died out in San Juan. The trees were old and those that remained tended to produce dark walnut meats rather than the preferred light. Earlier in the year walnut growers had closed their storage shed along the tracks north

This is a 1941 aerial view of San Juan Capistrano looking northwest.
Dark rows are orange groves and light rows are walnut groves.
Courtesy of Bill and Virginia Webb

Future Farmers of America 1940-45. Roy Ard, first in top row, Tony Plarcom, 3rd from left in middle row, and Fred Deere in bottom row.
Courtesy of the San Juan Capistrano Historical Society

disloyal to the United States, the War Department persuaded President Roosevelt to authorize the evacuation of some 112,000 west coast Japanese to so-called relocation centers which were actually prison camps," wrote Samuel Eliot Morrison and Henry Steele Commager in *The Growth of the American Republic*. Prior to the relocation other events took place. In San Juan, the constable was ordered to visit every Japanese family and confiscate their weapons. It didn't matter that he knew them and could vouch for their loyalty.

of the depot and decided to ship through Irvine. There was still cattle, wheat, truck crops, and fruit raised in the area, and the need for workers had not diminished.

As the war intensified, so did emotionalism. Patriotism was sometimes carried too far. People were nervous. Mysterious submarines were reported off the coast of Santa Barbara. A strange number of planes passed one night over Los Angeles. The newspapers were filled with battles won and battles lost. The soil was right for seeds of suspicion, and the harvest was a severe breach in the closeness that had characterized San Juan's past, a closeness that had, for a time, included Capistrano's Japanese citizens.

San Juan Capistrano had several families of Japanese ancestry living in or near town. Most were farmers. They were friendly, their children attended local schools, and they were involved in community activities, but like many people whose ancestors were from other countries, cultural ties were strong. In a time when patriotism reached fire and brimstone levels, this link with the past was misunderstood.

"Alarmed by the supposed danger of a Japanese attack on the Pacific Coast and fearful that persons of Japanese ancestry might prove

The author, Pamela, in 1947
Courtesy of the San Juan Capistrano Historical Society

Mrs. Ewardsen 6th Grade Class in 1951.
Courtesy of former Orange County Sheriff Brad Gates who is the 3rd person to the left in the 2nd row.

It was a government edict.

Most San Juan residents who were present during the spring of 1942 remember the Japanese relocation. Many were angered by the order; others frankly admit that at the time it seemed wise. One resident explained that many Japanese farmers were extremely enterprising. They had leased land at a low cost in places that most other farmers rejected, under power lines and near utility plants. Given the climate of emotionalism, these locations began to appear suspicious. By March, applications were being taken from farmers who wanted to take over the cultivation of the crops on Japanese property. Local residents were appointed to advise regional governing bodies all over California on who should get land. Les Remmers, who sat on the local advisory body, explained that the local group tried to

recommend only individuals who were familiar with the raising of the particular crops planted, so as to protect the productivity of the land. "I tried to be as impartial as possible," he recalled. "It was still a deplorable situation."

By May 15, all the Japanese were gone. Those who had remained in their homes as long as possible were notified through posters that they would be transported to camps.

Most of the Orange County Japanese population were taken to Parker Dam in Arizona. When a Supreme Court decision allowed some American citizens of Japanese ancestry to return to their homes this notice appeared on the editorial pages of the local newspaper:

"There has been a number of protests filed against the action of allowing Japanese to return to about their gardens, the quality of education in the schools, the weather, and who was buying and selling land. An occasional bizarre incident occurred to give people something else to think about. In July of 1942, J. H. McLeod of San Juan Capistrano filed suit in Santa Ana charging the Orange County Sheriffs Office with using fortune tellers to solve its cases. Two women — French Mary of Wintersburg and Madame Maxwell of Anaheim — were named in the suit. In August, it was reported that a 96-stick cache of dynamite was found buried near the local power plant. In September, people read about the latest exploits of the "strange, giant creature — half man and half ape — that has been seen walking with a lumbering gait near Stanton."

The most bizarre incident of all was an unannounced visit from the President of the United States. On September 25, a special train pulled into the Capistrano Depot. No prior notice was given on the time of arrival, purpose of visit, or ultimate destination. No special notice was to be taken of it. The visit of a President during war time was top secret. Nothing out of the ordinary should take place to note his presence.

By early morning, long before he arrived, everyone in town knew he was coming. Rumors began circulating when a large contingent of soldiers jumped off trucks and began to station themselves along the railroad tracks, at road crossings, and other strategic points in the city. If there were any remaining doubts, they were dispelled when machine guns were placed on top of prominent buildings. There was also a large number of men in suits conferring with the groups of highway patrolmen and sheriff's deputies. By the time the secret visitor pulled into the station and entered his long black limousine everyone in town had lined the streets waiting for a glimpse of Franklin Delano Roosevelt. The car proceeded up Verdugo to Camino Capistrano, circled the mission once, paused at the corner to be blessed by Father Hutchinson, and went on to Camp Pendleton. Two weeks later the secret service finally allowed the local paper to publicize the event.

The following year San Juan residents made a special trip to Camp Pendleton to take part in a dedication ceremony which would permanently place a part of San Juan Capistrano into the huge facility. It was the dedication of their depot bell. "Dedicated

Richard J. and Marguerite O'Neill were the owners of Rancho Mission Viejo, which employed many people from San Juan Capistrano.
Courtesy of the Rancho Mission Viejo

the west coast by different organizations, but a recent decision of the Supreme Court leaves no other action possible... As true American citizens, let us judge each returning Japanese as an individual, give him an opportunity to show his loyalty to this country. If a good job has been done in choosing those who may return to this section, there should be no trouble. If they have failed in their selections, there is apt to be many complications."

While the war disrupted the lives of many, it did not substantially alter the lives of most residents of San Juan Capistrano. People were still concerned

Father Arthur J. Hutchinson, Pastor of the mission for many years, started the St. Joseph's Day celebration on a formal basis.
Courtesy of Carmen Oyharzabal

who left on their honeymoon by train. It was last rung in 1914 to celebrate the wedding of Delfina Manriquez to William Olivares, at which time it was rung so hard that the bell cracked and was not used again. It remained in the belltower until Yorba heard that the commanding general at Camp Pendleton was restoring the old rancho buildings on the property. At that time Yorba wrote to him and told him the bell belonged to Camp Pendleton, and Santa Fe graciously gave it up.

By the end of 1943, the war effort seemed more hopeful and the aircraft warning program was discontinued. Boys began returning home and most of them were in great demand as speakers. Talent shows for servicemen were organized at nearby camps, and dances were still popular, particularly the ones held at the Blue Goose packing house. But the war was nearing a close. On April 17, 1945, San Juan residents picked up their weekly paper and read about the end of the war which they'd already heard on their radios a few days before. Rejoicing was private and public. Attention could now turn to other matters. The community had learned many things about itself during the war years, some good, and some bad. Yet a fundamental lesson was that the community could work together, in spite of personal views, for the public good.

As if sensing a new mood, the Archdiocese of Los Angeles in 1946 purchased the entire row of

as a symbol of peace for which Marines are fighting, a 115-year-old mission bell Sunday afternoon was returned to Camp Pendleton," reported the local paper, which said the bell would "forever remain a reminder of traditions which have made California great."

The bell, which had hung in the Capistrano Depot bell tower since 1894, was given to Santa Fe by Judge Richard Egan. According to Alfonso Yorba, the bell was brought to San Juan by Teodosio Belardes, in 1887 from a mission station once located at Las Flores. It remained in the possession of Judge Egan until the station was built and then placed in the tower. The bell was cast in 1828 at the Holbrook foundry in Massachusetts. Father Antonio Peyri bought the bell from a Yankee ship in exchange for hides. The bell hung in the depot tower and was rung vigorously for wedding parties

The Blue Goose label was the trademark of San Juan Capistrano American Fruit Growers packing house
Courtesy of the San Juan Capistrano Historical Society

American Fruit Growers Inc. - June 26, 1950
Front row: Adel Luna Velasquez, Grace Sepulveda Paramo, Tillie Serrano, Bertha Yorba, ---, ---, ---, ---
Second row: Veta Arce, Bernice Doram Jim, Delphina Manriquez Olivares, Sadee Sanchez, Louisa Manriquez Nieblas,
Jean Daneri, Rita Arce Nieblas, Albert Dyne, Clem Kelly, ---, ---, ---
Third row: Trini Villegas, Freeda Alarcon Camarena, ---, Josie Manriquez Olivares, Dora Stanfield, Dorothy Stanfield
Geolito, ---, ---, ---, ---
Fourth row: ---, ---, J. Wilcoxen, Norris Weatherholt, ---, ---, ---, Billie Speer, Bill White (hand on shoulder) John Sommers,
Reggie Nieblas
Courtesy of the San Juan Capistrano Historical Society

lots across from the mission on Ortega Highway. The reason quoted in the local paper was "to insure the character of the businesses facing the mission." The purchase included the land and buildings fronting Ortega Highway from El Camino Real to Camino Capistrano and those on Camino Capistrano physically attached to the block on Ortega Highway. Known as the Ferris Kelly block, the buildings had been built in the mid-1920s. The price quoted in the *Coastline Dispatch* was $125,000. Several years before, the archdiocese had purchased a block of buildings on El Camino Real from Ortega Highway south, including three adobes. The plans at the time of the purchase were to restore the building's early mission architecture and to construct a few other buildings, landscaping the

entire area with plants and shrubs similar to those on the mission grounds, according to an account in the local paper. Two buildings were restored but the third was torn down.

The year 1946 was not only a good year for restoration, it was also a good year for orange growers. During the month of July, the packing house reported that in one day the crews set a house record, packing thirty-eight hundred boxes, representing seven carloads of fruit. The fruit had been picked by ninety Mexican nationals. Braceros (imported farm workers) had been used in the area since the war years when the labor market was depleted.

It was also a good year for home builders, if they could find available land. Returning servicemen

Here is a birdseye view of an airplane approaching the runway at Capistrano Airport, looking northwest toward Dana Point. The airport was originally on the north side of San Juan Creek, west of Del Avion. The second airport opened in early 1960s across the creek.
Courtesy of Fred Stoffel

needed housing and many who had left the Capistrano Valley to join the armed forces came home with wives. While North Orange County erupted into a building boom, there was very little land for sale locally. Farmers in South County were not eager to sell to developers; their taxes weren't too high and farm prices were rising. But there were seven acres of flat vacant land right on the corner of El Camino Real and Acjachema streets, next to a residential district. Unfortunately, this was going to become the high school's new athletic field.

On April 26, San Juan residents learned that petitions were being circulated to subdivide the proposed field. "The school district recently received $1,000 from the Federal Works Agency to be used in making the preliminary plans for the athletic field; but many of our citizens feel that the property would be more suitable for residences," reported the *Coastline Dispatch*. According to the petition, signed by 115 citizens, "The future development of

San Juan Capistrano is being held back by not using this property for residences." The school board didn't agree. They kept their land and when funds became available, they put in their track and football

The first Capistrano Airport was opened in 1946 and was run by Fred Stoffel and Bill Webb.
Courtesy of Fred Stoffel

Planes were used for recreation and for instruction.
Courtesy of Fred Stoffel

Local flyers using the first Capistrano Airport were from left, Cisty Forster, Buddy Forster, Evelyn Forster, Charlotte Calhoun, Larry Buchheim, Cleo Forster, Pancho Forster, and Fred Stoffel.
Courtesy of Fred Stoffel

field. Today it is called Buchheim Field.

Another area was found for San Juan Capistrano's first postwar housing tract. It was on the southern edge of the downtown area north of San Juan Creek. It was called the Stoffel tract and by 1950, the second unit was being built. This new housing area provided homes for returning veterans and established residents alike. The town was beginning to grow. According to the 1950 census, 5,130 persons resided in San Juan Township. This was double the 1940 census which had tabulated only 2,432. The "township" boundaries were not the same as the city limits we know today. It included a much larger area. The San Juan Township boundaries, which Constable Carl Stroschein patrolled from 1937 to 1953, included El Toro on

This Victorian house on Del Avion was built in the 1890s by the Thomas family and is today owned by Evelyn Forster.
Courtesy of the First American Title Insurance Company

the north, the San Juan Hot Springs on the east, the county line on the south (except for San Clemente, which was incorporated) and the ocean on the west as far as south Laguna. The population of the town itself in 1950 was around 800.

Although the town was primarily an agricultural community, light industry was beginning to establish itself. In 1946, the Capistrano Ceramics Company, located on the southwest corner of El Camino Real and Ortega Highway, employed twenty-five people. In 1951, the Brad Keeler Artwares firm built a pottery plant south of the Judge Egan house. It, too, employed local people. The major employer was still the American Fruit Growers, but individual business firms in the downtown area were growing. These businessmen were again awaken-

This picturesque barn was once located adjacent to the Evelyn Forster home on Del Avion.
Courtesy of the San Juan Capistrano Historical Society

Judge Marco F. "Tom" Forster held court in the Avila Adobe on Camino Capistrano during the 1940s.
Courtesy of the San Juan Capistrano Historical Society

ing to Capistrano's heritage. Speakers before service groups spoke of the need to emphasize San Juan's past in architecture and the need for something like a yearly pageant to draw tourists to the area. To put these ideas into programs, the San Juan Capistrano Businessmen's Association was formed. Its members met at 6:00 a.m. at the Walnut Grove Cafe (then on Camino Capistrano). In later years this group would change its name to the Chamber of Commerce, but during the early 1950s, it kept its own name and annually put on a highly successful chuck wagon breakfast. It was also the first group to organize a formal fiesta in honor of the return of the swallows.

San Juan Capistrano at mid-century was still a small, socially-oriented town whose people belonged to the Woman's Club, Rotary, American Legion, and Lions' Club. Church groups were very active, the Sportsmen's Club still held annual turkey shoots, and the volunteer firemen's barbecue was a big event each year. The fifties would set the stage for the awakening of San Juan from close-knit village to sprawling little city. The fifties would be the last decade of comparative isolation and the sense of community would perhaps never be stronger.

While representatives in Congress were beginning to notice the speeches of a Senator named McCarthy, the big issue in San Juan was whether to put in street lights. Arguments flared on both sides.

Lighting the downtown area and residential streets around it would deter crime, argued the proponents; paying for them would break the taxpayers, countered the opponents. The vote was held in January of 1951 and the ayes won, 146 to 45; fifty-one street lights were ordered installed.

A national issue was taking the spotlight during this time, a war in far-off Korea. But the enthusiasm present during World War II was lacking in San Juan Capistrano's war effort. Few responded to pleas from the Orange County defense coordinator to again man an aircraft warning tower. The old one had been dismantled and another had to be erected outside of town. "The Korean War seems far off and remote," said an editorial in the *Coastline Dispatch*, "Yet many from Capistrano are fighting there." The editorial was remembered when on September 22, 1950, it was reported that Arnold Lobo was missing in action. In January, the town learned he had died.

The Lobos were a prominent family in San Juan Capistrano. Tracing their ancestry to the Juaneño Indians, members of the Lobo family had assumed leadership of the remaining Juaneños and had fought for their rights in Washington, D.C. In 1946, Clarence Lobo was elected chief of the Juaneños. He represented them before official government bodies and frequently spoke about Indian rights before local clubs. In a speech before the Rotary in July of 1951, he pointed out that in 1850, eighteen treaties were signed with California Indians, but Juaneños were left out. For that reason they were never included in a reservation or compensated for land. He hoped to correct the situation and see that Indians were given their fair share for land that was once theirs. The rights of Indians are championed today both by the Juaneño Band of Mission Indians, headed by David Belardes, and by the Capistrano Indian Council, a group organized in 1974 under the leadership of Jasper Hostler and Julian Ramos. Both groups' emphasis has been to help people of Indian ancestry learn about their history and culture, to take advantage of educational and employment opportunities, and to see that they obtain all benefits

Capistrano Union High School graduates - June 1944
Back row: Norman Haven, Armando Altamirano, Mr. Malcolm, James Bennett, John Lamb, Jack Molitor, Bernie Thedero, Mrs. Van Meter, Dale Weatherholt, Cliff Boessler. Middle row: Beverly Milner, Julie Jackson, Betty Ray, Barbara Cowger, Jerry Strang, June Nichols, Virginia Speer. Front row: Chris Glover, Patty Gibson, Eva Goodwin, Ida Jiminez, Marcia Draddy, Gertrude Gregg, Pat Welton.
Courtesy of Virginia Webb

for which they are eligible.

One of the most colorful of the Juaneños was Jose de Gracia Cruz, known locally as Acu, whom some believe was the last full-blooded Juaneño to live in San Juan Capistrano. Acu was the mission bellringer and was a featured character in *Capistrano Nights*. A skilled craftsman, Acu was known throughout the area for his reins and bridles which he made in his own yard, first tanning the hides and then cutting them into strips. According to Father O'Sullivan's account, Acu often had a waiting list for his wares and because he believed in taking his time, his customers sometimes waited a year for their orders. Acu was not only a craftsman, he was also a talented flutist, playing in an Indian orchestra which also included violins, bass violins, tambourines, a triangle, and drums. Unfortunately, he once fell with the flute into some mud and for a reason known only to him he never played again.

In April of every year Acu had a very special job, according to *Capistrano Nights*. He was the captain of the sheep shearers who came from Rincon and Pala to help with the work, his job being to oversee the workers. But he is most widely known for his tale about the swallows. Acu, conversing with Father O'Sullivan one day, told him where he thought the swallows came from, a story printed in *Capistrano Nights*:

The first year of the Fiesta de las Golondrinas Parade, as we now know it, was 1960. Celebrations in honor of the swallows' return began as early as the 1930s.
Courtesy of the First American Title Insurance Company

"They say, padre, that when they go away from here at summer's end, they fly to Jerusalem and stay there through the winter. I don't know why, but that is what people say ... and after that they come back here again for the feast of St. Joseph, and to build their little houses in the mission."

"But Acu," said I, "Between here and Jerusalem is a great ocean. How can they fly so far without getting tired and falling into the water?"

"You see padre," he replied very deliberately, "they carry with them in their beaks a little twig of a tree, and when they get tired flying across the ocean they put the twig on the water and alight

Clarence Lobo, Chief of the Juaneños is dressed in the traditional garb of Midwest Indian.
Courtesy of the San Juan Capistrano Historical Society

Acu, Jose de Gracia Cruz is believed to be last full-blooded Juaneño Indian.
Courtesy of the San Juan Capistrano Historical Society

town's uniqueness, its survival through two centuries, and the presence of families who could trace their ancestry to the mission's beginnings. Such continuity was a source of pride, yet it would be incorrect to say there was never discrimination or antagonism between Anglo-Americans and the native-born Californios. During the periods when Spanish was the dominant language, there was sometimes suspicion, mistrust, and prejudice displayed toward the handful of Anglos who lived in the community, and when English became the dominant language the situation reversed itself. Yet there was never the bitterness or the class distinctions that were found in border towns or big city barrios. Most of the people who were born and raised in Capistrano, whatever their cultural background, transcended pseudo barriers and thought of each other as individuals, rather than classes or groups. These same people say today that whatever prejudice existed, it was usually brought in by outsiders.

The fifties was a decade when many changes took place. One of these changes was the coming of the freeway.

For two hundred years San Juan Capistrano had been on the main road between San Diego and Los Angeles, serving as a convenient rest stop for

upon it and rest themselves."

Acu was known for his wit, his knowledge of a few words of the original language spoken in the area, and for his knowledge of Native American culture. Acu died in 1924, predicting accurately the date of his death.

The activities of the Juaneños thirty years after the death of Acu served to remind people of their heritage. They were again told of their

The freeway opened in 1959 and many thought the community was doomed.
Courtesy of the First American Title Insurance Company

Here is a view of Camino Capistrano looking north toward the mission in 1959.
Courtesy of the San Juan Capistrano Historical Society

One, on La Calera, was the first house to be wired for electricity. It had; been moved to the site from a downtown location. Another was an adobe which some believed dated back to 1794, although in fact it was built in 1874 by James Sheehan, a settler from Montana. It was located south of Ortega Highway near the El Homo barranca. When it was taken down, it was noted that it had an old-style roof made of straw, and the thick adobe walls still carried the imprint of human fingers which fashioned them. The state was willing to move it, but

travelers by horse, wagon, stagecoach, and finally, the automobile. There was only one road going north and south through San Juan, and as towns grew between the two metropolitan centers, more and more cars traveled the highway until traffic jams, particularly on weekends and in the summer, were a common occurrence. It was therefore no surprise to read in the papers in July of 1952 that the Santa Ana Freeway might be extended through El Toro. The news was, at the same time, disquieting. When would it be extended further? How close would it come to the town? How great would its impact be? Everyone had his own answer. The freeway was a destroyer or a deliverer; an intrusion or progress with a capital P.

In October, the proposed route through San Juan Capistrano was presented to the Businessmen's Club. It would follow the old highway to Trabuco Bridge, would swing northeast of the downtown area, and would rejoin the highway at San Juan Creek. The route jangled a few. It would be too close to town, too close to the elementary school. Reroute it, they said, through Mission Viejo Ranch. The following February the route was accepted by the Orange County Board of Supervisors.

Freeway construction began early in 1957 and several houses were removed from its path.

Here is the bandits trysting tree on Junipero Serra Road. The freeway offramp was relocated to keep it.
Courtesy of the San Juan Capistrano Historical Society

experts decided that it could not be moved, so it was destroyed.

Another landmark threatened by a freeway access road was saved, but it took Machiavellian strategy and Capistrano storytelling to do it. It was the trysting tree.

"If the ghost of Joaquin Murietta has a sense of humor, it must be having a chuckle at the irony of a group of San Juan Capistrano citizens who are doing their best to convince an unfeeling highway department that Murietta's Sycamore should be spared by the onrush of the freeway," reported the *Coastline Dispatch*. "The large sycamore, which local legend

Twin-Winton Ceramics building operated on Camino Capistrano south of the Egan House for many years. It was torn down in the early 1980s. Brad Keeler Artware preceded it. Courtesy of the San Juan Capistrano Historical Society

has long identified as a trysting spot for the dashing bandit on his trips to the old mission town, at one time had Murietta's name carved in its base, but it has gradually been obscured by the growing giant, until only a scar remains." The fight to save the tree was led by Carl Buchheim, who later became San Juan's first mayor. Armed with a petition, he and several other citizens personally contacted members of the state highway commission and convinced them the tree should be spared. The state officials were not as unfeeling as predicted. Because saving the tree required only the relocation of an access route (Junipero Serra Street) and not the freeway itself, the request was granted.

Still standing on the north side of Junipero Serra, the tree is somewhat of a mystery. Although a local story persists that Murietta indeed visited Capistrano, primarily to rest and hide in the secret attic room of the Rios Adobe, his biographers don't believe he came this far south. On the other hand, the biographers of the "Robin Hood of the West" disagree on several points, particularly what happened to him. According to some accounts, Murietta was killed, decapitated, and his head (pickled in a glass jar) taken on tour to be displayed

in carnival side shows. It was last seen in a saloon in San Francisco before the earthquake. Other accounts claim that the person killed was not really Murietta, but one of a number of bandits who were called Joaquin whose crimes were blamed on Murietta. These believe that Murietta escaped and went to Mexico, never to return. Dan Rios, a descendant of Gregorio Rios, who knew Murietta, said his family always believed he escaped. To prove it he once took a trip deep into Baja to the place where Murietta supposedly settled. There he found many people who claimed to be his descendants.

The mystery of Murietta is not the only one to touch the tree. In a publication called *The Capistrano Story*, historian Bill Smith calls the tree the "Tiburcio Vasquez tree," describing it as the place this bandit met his gang. Murietta is not mentioned, and it isn't surprising. The story about the famous bandit's use of the tree as a trysting place was concocted one morning in a downtown coffee shop by some well-meaning gentlemen who could not understand why the highway department had to take out a beautiful old tree when they could easily move the road two feet. Fortified with the idea that the end justified the means, they launched a campaign to convince everyone that the tree had

Jean Goodwin Ames created this design for a mural out of tiles for Twin-Winton Ceramics when it opened on Camino Capistrano. The mural is now part of Mercado Village, built at the same location.
Courtesy of the San Juan Capistrano Historical Society

historical significance. They did their work so well that a state delegation came to town armed with a bronze plaque destined for the tree. The ceremony, however, never took place. Someone boldly told the state officials that the tree had no historical value and they left in a huff. Fortunately, the road had already been moved. The tree still stands and if it had no historical significance before, it has now. No one can prove that bandits trysted there, but historians will from now on be able to point to the tree and say "it was one of the biggest bits of chicanery ever put over on the State Highway Department."

As work on the freeway continued, people began to wonder about its long-range effect on the town. Some said it would have none, while others thought the effects would be overwhelming.

"The new freeway linking this area with the already present freeways to the north will bring added population," reported the local paper. "We are playing ostrich to assume the vast growth of Southern California is going to completely pass us by."

Growth would indeed come, but no one knew how much or how soon. And in the fifties there were still some who doubted it would come at all. They looked at other towns the freeway had killed, towns whose business districts had become shells with the loss of main-highway-through-town

traffic, and they feared this would happen to San Juan Capistrano. They didn't realize that five acres of insurance stood in the middle of town, five acres of beauty and tradition that had stood for two hundred years as a symbol of faith and would stand for many years after, quietly influencing the town that bears its name. Yet soon after the freeway opened everyone knew it.

"This weekend's influx of tourists proves one thing," said the local paper in January of 1959, a few weeks after the opening of the freeway. "In spite of the freeway, people will continue to flock to San Juan Capistrano. Their primary interest is in the old mission."

Though coming as a surprise to some, during most of the twentieth century San Juan Capistrano businessmen had been aware of the economic value of the town's past. Some had capitalized on it, giving Spanish names to their restaurants and stores or a Spanish look to their exterior facades. Others had not. But in the fifties recognition of the town's marketability heightened. Where it had been optional to be a Spanish village before, it now seemed imperative to many. People were coming to Capistrano to see the mission, to immerse themselves in the spirituality and culture of the past. To keep them in town a little longer, the town would have to extend the flavor of the mission beyond its walls.

A modest attempt to attract tourists to town

had been launched in 1956 by James DiMaio, who had spearheaded an advertising program which placed billboards on major highways. The billboards, one of which still stands on the roof of the Capistrano Trading Post, said "follow the swallows to Capistrano." In 1959, when the thousands of cars from the freeway helped pinpoint San Juan's attraction in the minds of the business community, the plans were more ambitious. In order to draw attention to the other aspects of the town, the Chamber of Commerce hired an artist

Capistrano Union High School's modern wing was added in 1938-1939. It is still standing today.
Courtesy of Mark Gibson

to study the downtown area and to prepare a "facelift" plan to make the buildings early Cali-

Ruins of the west wing of the mission are shown here prior to reconstruction.
Courtesy of the San Juan Capistrano Historical Society

This is a view of the west wing of the mission during reconstruction in 1959.
Courtesy of the San Juan Capistrano Historical Society

Here are buildings on the west side of Camino Capistrano, shown through a doorway at the mission. Courtesy of the San Juan Capistrano Historical Society

signs of disease and older trees were not producing well. Some had already been taken out. When the plant closed, growers who continued to farm citrus crops had to ship their oranges through Santa Ana area packing houses. Walnuts were completely gone. Truck farming continued on a small scale and cattle still roamed the hills of the O'Neill Ranch, but other types of agriculture had dwindled and died. Ceramics plants, many of which had changed hands several times, were still alive but tourism had reached major importance in the survival of the town.

The magnet for tourists, the mission, was not standing still. In 1951, the community was saddened by the death of Father Arthur J. Hutchinson, who had come to the mission in the thirties. In October of 1951, the town welcomed a new pastor, the Rt. Rev. Msgr. Vincent Lloyd-

Landscaping, much of it planted during Father O'Sullivan's time, makes San Juan the "jewel of the missions." Courtesy of the San Juan Capistrano Historical Society

fornian in appearance. Mrs. Otheto Weston was hired to take on the project. The idea was backed by a petition drive to encourage the Board of Supervisors to create an architectural control committee to advise them on San Juan Capistrano projects, and later that spring, the chamber formulated a promotion plan designed to attract tourists. Among suggestions for the coming summer was the designation of four weekends for special entertainment, the resurrection of the central plaza in the downtown area, and the construction of a bandstand. That year, the seventh annual chuckwagon breakfast drew record crowds, and one month later, the new Don Juan Fiesta drew two thousand.

Tourism was, at this point, San Juan's major industry. The American Fruit Growers packing house had closed at the end of the 1952 season. Orange trees in San Juan were beginning to show

The mission forecourt has always been a focal point for its beautiful gardens.
Courtesy of the San Juan Capistrano Historical Society

Russell, a scholar whose deep interest in the past gave the mission new vigor. An expert on Shakespeare, the Monsignor was former dean of the English Department of Loyola University of Los Angeles. He was born in Ireland and held degrees in anthropology and archaeology from the University of Southern California. Under his leadership, an expanded school opened on the mission grounds followed by a new parish hall and gymnasium. Sidewalks were installed on the east and west sides of the mission and restoration work begun on the almost totally ruined western section of the mission quadrangle. The work was supervised by Jay Latham, who hand carved some of the beams and incorporated one of the original arches which was still standing into the newly reconstructed buildings. Latham used old maps and drawings and studied the other parts of the original mission structures to guide him in the restoration, though the bricks used are a specially treated adobe which will withstand the elements. Corridor arches were rebuilt, using as much of the original as possible, but the original floor of the west wing was not saved because of modern building codes.

In addition to the work on the west wing of the quadrangle, other parts of the mission were also renovated and repaired so that they, too, would last another two hundred years. The Serra Chapel was repainted so that it looked as it did in the past, the chapel's statuary was renovated, and the reredos (the ornate background of the altar) was redone. Because of the Monsignor's interest in education, an eight-scene diorama depicting the life and times of the mission was added to the rear of the mission quadrangle especially for children.

Adults as well as children began to visit the mission in increasing numbers in the 1950s, particularly after the freeway opened. Predictions that the freeway would bring growth as well as visitors began to come true. Those who needed reassurance had only to pick up their weekly paper to find it.

"The subject of San Juan Capistrano's future is always good for a discussion among its residents and on more than one occasion opinions have reached a deadlock," proclaimed an editorial in 1959. "There are those who predict great things for the mission town and many who have put forth a real effort to cultivate progress for the community. On the other hand, there are those who hotly deny such progress will come about for this community as it has so overwhelmingly for other Orange County rural areas. These nonbelievers often acted with vengeance against even preparing for the future in the event that progress does come to this quiet mission valley. A good point on the progress side of the argument can be seen in the new direct-dial system installed in the new building on El Camino Real. Apparently, Pacific Telephone and Telegraph Company has faith in the inevitable growth of the area or it wouldn't have spent $130,000 to locate the installation in San Juan Capistrano."

The sixties and seventies would be decades of rapid change and bitter struggle. Old fights — importation of water and location of the high school — would be settled. New battles over growth, land use, and government control would be waged. But out of the turmoil a new sense of identity would emerge, a new interest in the remnants of San Juan Capistrano's past, and a new awareness of their fragility in the hands of man.

John Malcom was the first principle of Capistrano Union High School. The district was formed in 1919 with high school classes first taught in a temporary building at San Juan School in 1920.

Courtesy of Barbara Baum

Here is an aerial view looking east over Capistrano Valley in the 1890s.
Courtesy of the San Juan Capistrano Historical Society

Chapter 8

Urbanization and the Bicentennial
1960 – 1976

"The problem with incorporation," wrote an opponent in 1933, "is that there would always be the danger of control slipping into the hands of visionary promoters who might run the people into debt and difficulty."

In the decade of the 1960s, incorporation was a major issue, but it was only one of many. While people across the nation fought verbal battles over Vietnam, social injustice, and the conservation of natural resources, people in San Juan turned their attention to the issue of local control and the articulation of traditional paradoxes: the retention of self-sufficiency versus the acceptance of outside aid; and the protection of the town's unique character sometimes at the expense of individual rights.

Historians have called the sixties a time of political reawakening. San Juan Capistrano reflected this theme, though problems that held national interest were not the subject of local political controversies. The arguments of the sixties were waged over local concerns that had been simmering for years and finally boiled over — importation of water, unification of schools, and the future of the community. San Juan residents were particularly concerned about two issues: the advisability of incorporation and the location of the new high school.

The school fight began earlier than 1960, its roots extending back to 1919 when the high school district was formed. At that time it included not only San Juan, which had a small community of residents, but areas that would become San Clemente, Dana Point, Capistrano Beach, Laguna Niguel, in addition to parts of the O'Neill Ranch

and areas east of the ranch, all of which were relatively unsettled. When the high school was built, the center of population was in Capistrano, but as the years passed, it gradually shifted to San Clemente, which had incorporated in 1928, and more and more school board members were elected from that city. While population centers changed, the school began to age. Repairs were made as needed, but by the late 1940s, it became apparent that an addition would be necessary. Some believed an entire new school should be built and with that thought voiced, the district embarked on one of the bitterest fights ever known in the Capistrano Valley.

In late 1955, a tax override election was passed and the board decided the money should be used to purchase a school site in the Palisades area overlooking Capistrano Beach. Unfortunately the override passed by only two votes and court injunctions were filed contesting the election. In February of 1956, the board announced that it would purchase a high school site in San Clemente. They would purchase forty acres for $1,500 an acre. In March the site, located on the Reeves Ranch, was rejected. In April a taxpayers' group was organized in San Juan Capistrano to protest moving the school out of town. If a new school had to be built, let it be built on the old site. San Clemente residents opposed this view. They claimed that the impetus for growth would be in their community and therefore, the new school should be located where the most population would be — San Clemente.

The school board, ignoring both sides, tried to compromise and in January of 1957, an-

This aerial view of Capistrano Valley is looking east in 1965. The white ribbon through center is Trabuco Creek Channel.
Courtesy of Shirley J. Adams

nounced they would file a condemnation suit on the site located between the two communities in the Capistrano Beach Palisades. But by August, the board had changed its mind and the suit was dropped. The mysterious dropping of the condemnation action was soon solved when on October 10, people read in their *Coastline Dispatch* that 32.5 acres would be purchased by the Capistrano Union High School District in northern San Clemente on land owned by Hugo Forster. The school would be called the

Williams Gym withstood pressures for removal until the late 1970s.
It stood where the San Juan Capistrano Regional Library is today.
Courtesy of the San Juan Capistrano Historical Society

150

Hugo Forster High School. People worked frantically behind the scenes; negotiations were stalled. In December, Forster asked that negotiations be stopped.

Battle lines, clearly drawn, continued to hold. In April of 1958, the school board decided to proceed with the Palisades site, continuing the condemnation suit. But the district had a severe problem. It had no money with which to purchase the site and construct the school, so in February, a $2 million bond election was held. It failed. In June, the district tried again to pass a bond issue and once again it failed, but by this time people were exceedingly angry and election tactics were tawdry enough to prompt an editorial in the *Coastline Dispatch* chastising both sides for their name calling and "dirty politics." The writer pointed out the need for new facilities and told opponents of the bond measure that they

The first City Hall building was rented space. It is seen through the Capistrano Depot arches after demolition of the Capistrano Hotel in the early 1960s.
Courtesy of the San Juan Capistrano Historical Society

would have to accept the responsibility for holding back local education.

To emphasize the point that the high school was no longer adequate, the board invited a state team to inspect the school in November of 1958. The team, whose purpose was to evaluate the safety of the buildings, stated that the administration building, seven classrooms, and the auditorium were unsafe and should be closed, but the gymnasium and arts building were satisfactory. The board took quick action. In December, the unsafe buildings were closed, a month later the school was on double sessions, and shortly after, the board ordered the purchase of quonset huts to ease overcrowding. But the prospects for the future looked dim. Although the Palisades land had been condemned, the district

During the 1970s, San Juan Capistrano was one of the fastest growing cities in the state. This view shows Ortega properties under construction.
Courtesy of the San Juan Capistrano Historical Society

This view of San Juan Capistrano is looking north from the hills above the golf course, showing a developing community. The general plan calls for protection of major ridgelines.
Courtesy of the San Juan Capistrano Historical Society

This olive press depicts functional tasks performed on the mission grounds during the Spanish period.
Courtesy of the San Juan Capistrano Historical Society

had failed to pass a bond issue to pay for the land. Perturbed by the worsening situation in San Juan Capistrano, an Orange County grand jury stepped in April of 1960.

While the grand jury was making its investigation, an advisory committee appointed by the school board recommended that the administration-auditorium building be replaced, that lockers be added to the gymnasium, new metal shop be built, and that the board should develop a master plan and purchase a new site. Taking the advice of their appointees, the board recommended the demolition of the auditorium building. At this point the grand jury released its report, which traced the activities of the district back to 1947. The problem with the district, said the report, was that it represented two distinct viewpoints. Voters in San Juan Capistrano wanted to retain the old school; voters elsewhere in the district wanted a more centrally located facility.

"Much bitterness has been created in the community which is unbecoming in any area," said the report. "It appears both sides stooped to unethical practices, all designed to foster their particular viewpoints. Unwillingness is evidenced with many we talked with to compromise at all. Others take a more realistic view and say there must be a compromise."

The conclusion of the report was that a package deal should be proposed to district voters, offering the renovation of the old site and the purchase of a new site. But the grand jury report came too late. Announcement of the proposed demolition

The tranquility of the mission is captured by its peaceful fountains. Courtesy of the San Juan Capistrano Historical Society

of the auditorium was like waving a red shirt in front of a corral of bulls. People were furious and a petition drive was immediately launched in San Juan to halt the coming destruction, while a counter-petition drive was started in San Clemente to support it. Both sides dug in; no one was prepared to listen to the grand jury's talk of a compromise. A tangible piece of San Juan Capistrano was in jeopardy and if that went, thought some, so would the rest of the school, and who knows what would be next.

The degree of emotionalism generated by the issue went deeper than the mere destruction of an old building. Knocking down the walls of a structure most people in San Juan had pride in was symbolic, not only of the long battle with San Clemente, but with the town's struggle to retain its community identity, to keep its self-sufficiency in a world which was beginning to encroach on the unique character of the oldest town in Orange County. Because of its implications for the future, people fought harder to keep the walls up and the wolf from the door, and on a hot day in August, they made their move.

The day began like any other except for the demolition crew which drove into town in the morning, stopping outside the auditorium-administration building. The first thing to do was to remove the shrubbery which skirted the structure. The day's plan settled, the crew began to work. Before long an angry crowd had gathered that began to mill around, shouting, chanting, making threats. The contractor, Corliss Pipher, heard them; his workmen were nervous, stopping from time to time to watch the crowd. A few grabbed uprooted shrubs and tried to put them back. There was talk that the main gas line had not been turned off and knocking down the building would therefore endanger the safety of the nearby residential district. Pipher stayed. He had a job to do. It wasn't his fault. He was only the contractor.

But if he remained, said unnamed persons, his equipment might be blown up. If he didn't leave, said the unnamed persons, he might be shot. Pipher no longer hesitated. He called the sheriff.

Silvas Adobe, located on Los Rios Street, has survived since 1794.
Courtesy of the San Juan Capistrano Historical Society

ordered the structure to be left untouched until the outcome of the suit.

During the next two years, in an attempt to follow the grand jury's advice, the Capistrano Union High School District attempted to pass a bond issue calling for the retention of the old high school and the purchase of a site for a new one. San Clemente residents wouldn't budge. They wanted a new high school built and the old one closed. In March of 1962, the board tried for the ninth time to get their school bond measure passed. It again failed and the board gave up on the compromise effort and late that same month, they announced a $2.5 million

The day did not end in a crash of walls or physical violence. At the final moment a group armed with a court injunction against the demolition arrived and halted the work. The injunction stated that the destruction was a "wanton waste of taxpayers' money because the building could be used for storage." The attorney for the Capistrano group also proved that an engineer had never declared the building unsafe, only a team of architects. In the meantime, a taxpayers' suit, filed by Boyd Robertson, sought to prevent the demolition of the building. The court

Here is the Avila Adobe as it looked when it was a dress shop called Nelly's in the 1970s. The building had been extensively remodeled at that time.
Courtesy of the San Juan Capistrano Historical Society

Domingo Yorba Adobe, dating back to the 1840s and the Oyharzabal family home since 1878, was listed by Orange County architects as a significant structure.
Courtesy of the San Juan Capistrano Historical Society

El Adobe, a restaurant since before World War II, was adapted from two 1840s structures: The Miguel "Chavito" Yorba Adobe on the north and the Juzgado Adobe on the south.
Courtesy of the San Juan Capistrano Historical Society

bond issue to build a new high school in San Clemente. In June, the election was held and the bonds passed. Capistrano lost.

The old buildings, the focal point for the fight between San Clemente and San Juan Capistrano, stood a few years longer, but they eventually came down, their walls annihilated by termites, and the community mourned

This photo depicts life in the Aguilar Adobe around 1910. Note the beehive oven in background.
Outdoor ovens were used in older adobes for cooking.
Courtesy of the San Juan Capistrano Historical Society

The Texaco station on the corner of Ortega Highway and El Camino Real was built on the site of Cañedo Adobe.
Courtesy of the San Juan Capistrano Historical Society

the loss. Capistrano Union High School graduated its last class in 1964. Later that year, the first unification election was held. It finally passed after several attempts, a unification which absorbed the historic San Juan Capistrano Elementary District but retained part of its name. The unification brought together the high school district and the elementary districts of San Juan, Capistrano Beach, and San Clemente. Today they are called Capistrano Unified School District.

At this writing, in 1990, the remaining buildings of the old high school, first used in 1939, still stand. But the gymnasium, built in 1928, was finally removed in the 1970s. Yet, something more permanent exists as a result of the fight over the original school. It is the word "city." There are many who believe that San Juan Capistrano would not have incorporated as soon if it had not been for the long fight over the location of the high school and the short, but emotional, fight over the old buildings. The struggle not only set the stage for incorporation, but set the mood. In mid-June of 1960, the school board, except for Betty

Forster, Capistrano's member, had voted to demolish the old structures. Only one month later five men, most of whom had been active in the school hassles, filed incorporation papers.

"Capistrano Valley Shocked By Sneak Incorporation Move," screamed the headline in the *Coastline Dispatch* on July 21, 1960. Five residents had taken out papers for incorporation of San Juan Capistrano — C. Fulton Shaw, Reginald Erickson, Henry Stewart, Carl Buchheim, and Larry Buchheim. The proponents told the newspaper they did it to "protect the area for 90 days," until a thorough study could be done. But the Coastline editor disapproved of the move, saying it had created distrust in Dana Point and Capistrano Beach.

People had been talking about incorporation since the late 1950s, looking at a tri-city concept which would include San Juan, Dana Point, and Capistrano Beach in one incorporated area. In April of 1960, the talk grew into action and in May, the Chamber of Commerce launched a full scale incorporation study. For that reason it came as a

A pile of bricks is all that remains of Cañedo Adobe. A picnic area is next to it on Ortega Highway, next to the Jack in the Box.
Courtesy of the San Juan Capistrano Historical Society

surprise to many to read that San Juan might incorporate by itself. The town had little industrial tax base, a small population (just over one thousand) and land that was mostly agricultural. It seemed more logical at the time to incorporate the three areas, but the high school fight, which represented the growing loss of local control, was still fresh in everyone's minds. And the fate of the

La Casa Grande, which housed the Las Rosas Restaurant until the 1960s, was torn down to make way for a bank.
Courtesy of the San Juan Capistrano Historical Society

old high school was not yet settled. It was a fortuitous time to get support for an idea that might otherwise have been resisted.

In August, the school issue came to a head and one month later, petitions began to be circulated for the incorporation of the town, an event characterized by the unsympathetic local paper as "an incident reminiscent of the fellow who got the wildcat by the tail and couldn't let go." Proponents had no trouble getting the required number of signatures,

for a few weeks later the boundary questions were settled (with people from Capistrano Beach and Dana Point successfully protesting the proposed boundaries which they thought too far-reaching). The boundaries were officially set by the Orange County Board of Supervisors in January of 1961, the incorporation election was scheduled for the following April, and proponents set out to sell the idea to the general public. In 1933, a group of citizens had tried to do the same thing, wanting to incorporate to crack down on peddlers, require outside firms to have licenses to conduct business in San Juan, and to insure local use of traffic fines. The reasons in 1961 were a little different, but the overall issue was still local control. Not only did the residents want a voice in planning their own future, they also feared that the county government might not always know what's best for the mission town. Proponents called themselves Neighbors of San Juan Capistrano for Incorporation, and their platform was to keep San Juan Capistrano's historic name intact, to place future growth in the hands of its citizens, to receive more direct benefit from tax dollars, and to prevent annexation by San Clemente (rumors flew that this was imminent). On April 11, 1961, by a vote of 358 for and 88 against, the town became a city.

The city's official birthday is April 19, the

A new Bank of America building was built in the 1960s on the Casa Grande site across from the El Adobe Restaurant.
Courtesy of the San Juan Capistrano Historical Society

Here is a view of Capistrano Depot looking north after the white stucco was sandblasted to reveal brick underneath.
Courtesy of the San Juan Capistrano Historical Society

council during its first six months was to oppose a grandiose plan of the county's to extend Ortega Highway from the mission to Del Obispo. Plans called for six lanes and would have destroyed much of the historic Los Rios area. Another action taken by the council was the establishment of an architectural control district in the area around the mission. This first district, set up to "preserve the historical area of the city, including not only the world-famous jewel of the missions itself, but also other structures in the area" included the area bounded by La Zanja, the San Diego Freeway, Del Obispo (from Ortega Highway to the Santa Fe Tracks), and the railroad tracks on the west. Today the district extends further, encompassing the entire business district of the city.

Two other momentous actions were taken, but both proved unpopular and were defeated. One was the annexation of the Capistrano Beach village district to provide a corridor to the sea, and the other was the hiring of a police

day the state declared the cityhood legal. Its first councilmen, elected on the same ballot as the incorporation measure, were Carl Buchheim (who subsequently was named mayor), William Bathgate, Don Durnford, Antonio Olivares, and Edward Chermak. The city's size was approximately six thousand acres and its population was estimated at twelve hundred. The new city's first staff members were Ernest Thompson, who became both administrator and clerk, and John Dawson, attorney. The first official City Hall was the brick building on the east side of Camino Capistrano a few yards south of the corner of Ortega Highway. It was then the vacant Conners' Department Store building and was rented to the city for $75 per month.

One of the first actions taken by the new council was to contract with the Orange County Sheriff's Office for police protection. The cost of the first contract service was $6,300 for the year. In 1975, it had risen to $298,500. To obtain revenue to run the new city, the council set a tax rate of sixty cents per $100 assessed valuation, but it rose in 1962 to ninety cents and remained at that level until 1978, when the tax structure was changed in California, and property taxes were no longer set by city councils. One of the first actions taken by the fledgling

Brad Gates, who grew up in San Juan Capistrano, was elected Sheriff of Orange County in 1974.
He is shown with President Ronald Reagan.
Courtesy of the San Juan Capistrano Historical Society

chief. The first was opposed by the county, the other was opposed by the citizens of the city who wanted to retain the services of the County Sheriff. Both incidents were controversial, but not bizarre, yet 1962 opened with an incident which was both controversial and bizarre, an incident which might have drastically altered the course of growth in San Juan Capistrano as it approached its two hundredth birthday.

C. Russell Cook Barn, built in 1898, has survived property sales and surrounding development and still stands today off Del Obispo Road.
Courtesy of the San Juan Capistrano Historical Society

In its early years, the city did not have a full planning department with a director, assistants, and secretaries. It didn't even have an office. "People would bring their plans down to the restaurant and show them to me," recalled the first Planning Commission Chairman Fred Newhart, Jr., owner of the Walnut Grove. "It was all very informal in those days."

One visitor to Newhart's restaurant was Ross Cortese. Cortese's project was mammoth

Orange groves began to pull out of the area as property taxes escalated and housing markets developed.
Courtesy of the San Juan Capistrano Historical Society

by San Juan standards. He planned to build a retirement community for senior citizens on 3,580 acres of the Moulton Ranch. The only problem was that his land, which he wanted to annex to San Juan, was nine miles away. Would San Juan, therefore, annex a strip of land alongside the San Diego Freeway from its northernmost boundary to Cortese's southernmost boundary? The developer wanted use of the city's name, use of its police and fire services, but the self-contained community would have its own water and sewer facilities.

"It was an interesting idea," recalled Newhart. "But folks had a lot of questions. Would those forty thousand new residents vote for our sewer and water bonds, having their own? Would they vote for our school bonds and tax overrides?"

Because of the numerous unanswered questions, the problem of strip annexation, and the newness of the city, the planning commission voted against the annexation. The city council followed suit, stating that it was outside the city's sphere of influence. Attorney John Dawson opposed the council's action. He told them they were making a mistake in turning down this chance to grow in stability and stature. But councilmen countered that most people wanted San Juan to remain a small town. A disappointed Cortese told them they were living in a dream

Kinoshita Farms has operated from this 1877 house built by Joel Congdon since the 1950s.
Corn and strawberries are major crops today.
Courtesy of the San Juan Capistrano Historical Society

but San Juan Terrace and Village, both on San Juan Creek Road, sprang up during this growth period. The 1960s was the decade for the construction of most of the mobile home parks, those off Alipaz, the ones off Aeropuerto, and Camino Capistrano. Alto Capistrano was begun in the 1960s as was Troy Homes, Village San Juan, and the Casas. The late 1960s and early 1970s found construction along the Ortega Highway and off Del Obispo. In the early 1970s, San Juan Capistrano was the fastest-growing city in the state. Ross Cortese's predictions had come true.

world. "These gentlemen on the planning commission are taking it for granted that the town is going to sleep," he said. "Your city is going to grow."

Cortese's plans were offered to other cities. Laguna Beach turned him down and though Santa Ana for a time seemed willing, those plans also fell through, and Leisure World Laguna Hills was built in unincorporated territory where it is today.

San Juan Capistrano did grow, almost overnight. The late 1960s and early years of the 1970s were ones of rapid, uninhibited growth. Orange groves were pulled out to make room for shopping centers and housing developments. Population figures soared from a little over a thousand in 1960 to 12,850 at the end of 1975. During this period all the housing developments on both sides of Camino Capistrano, from the mission north to Junipero Serra, were built and occupied. San Juan Park was built in the late 1950s,

One of the things that helped the city to grow was the availability of Metropolitan Water. But importation of water was a controversial subject dur-

The Olivares House on Los Rios Street was privately restored by Gil Jones.
Courtesy of the San Juan Capistrano Historical Society

160

ing the 1950s when the town was still small and many residents thought it would remain that way. Talk of bringing Metropolitan Water to the Capistrano Valley began in the late 1940s, but at that point it was just talk. The downtown business and residential areas were served by wells. Water quality wasn't the best, but it was passable, so why bring it all the way from the Colorado River? Farmers, in particular, were against the idea. Most had their own wells and irrigation systems. Importing water would be costly. They just couldn't afford it. But the talk continued and in September of 1951, action was taken, meetings organized, battles waged, but nothing happened. The issue cooled off and was temporarily forgotten. Behind the scenes, plans quietly continued and two years later boundary lines were proposed for the Southern Orange County Water District which would import Metropolitan Water. Ranchers protested; bitter words flew, and San Juan Capistrano quietly withdrew.

This cottage at the rear of the Olivares House was completely rebuilt to resemble the original building.
Courtesy of the San Juan Capistrano Historical Society

The issue simmered for a few years with nothing done until 1958, when it once again came to a head. Again it was opposed, but proponents refused to drop it. In 1960, Capistrano was given its last chance. San Clemente, Dana Point, and Capistrano Beach had all voted to bring in Metropolitan Water. If San Juan was to join in payment for the pipeline, they would have to join now. If voters turned it down this time and wanted to join later, the cost would be greatly increased.

"It was not the cost of the actual water that worried people," said T. J. Meadows, then manager of Orange County Waterworks District No. 4. "It was the cost of the pipeline to bring the water into the area." In August, a committee was formed, headed by Les Remmers, to sell the idea to the public. The water was needed for consumption; farmers could still drill wells and irrigate their crops with local water. Unfortunately, the number of dissolved solids in the local water was increasing and would soon be unfit to drink. The vote was held

Branding cattle on the O'Neill Ranch in the 1960s.
Courtesy of the San Juan Capistrano Historical Society

Rodeo time on the O'Neill Ranch calls for branding and roping several thousand steers.
Courtesy of the San Juan Capistrano Historical Society

the following November with 356 people voting in favor and fifty-six against bringing Metropolitan Water to San Juan Capistrano. With a supply of good water insured and sewer bonds passed (late in the 1960s) the new city was ready to meet the needs of the future.

Why did the town grow so fast in the sixties? While many thought the freeway would sound San Juan's death knell, it had in fact done the opposite. Capistrano had very little industry itself, but it was now only a short distance from Santa Ana and other major employment centers. People no longer felt the need to work in the community they lived in and in the 1960s, when urban centers were in a state of unrest, people began to look for suburban environments in which to live and raise their families. San Juan Capistrano, which had preserved its quiet, mission village character and was ideally located next to a freeway, was what many people sought. Some people claim that developers cast covetous eyes on the virgin hills and valleys of San Juan and immediately called in the bulldozers and public relations men. Others claim that the growth of San

Juan was inevitable, that it was a natural outgrowth of the boom of Orange County. Aiding the boom were changes in the tax structure which decreed that property was to be taxed according to its highest and best future use, rather than its actual use. Because it was a constant gamble to farm crops which depended on the weather for their success, many ranchers decided to sell rather than continue to pay high taxes on land that might not be profitable to farm.

There was another factor, one less tangible, but probably just as important, and that was the town itself. During a time of national restlessness, San Juan Capistrano represented stability and endurance. It was a town whose roots stretched two hundred years, and at its center was a symbol of permanence, the mission. In a period when student unrest, riots in city ghettos, and the daily horrors of war-filled newspapers and television screens, San Juan Capistrano must have seemed an oasis untouched by the grim realities of the outside world. It was a city of the past where century-old ideals could still be found enshrined within the walls of

162

the mission, where cattle-covered hills changed with the seasons, and trees reached for the sky. To shut out the present, if only for a moment, one had only to sit beside the fountain in the old mission quadrangle where the trickling water and the silence of growing flowers tranquilized the senses and prepared the soul for peace. With eyes closed, one could imagine Indians working in the courtyard, skillfully tying lengths of rawhide into lariats, with little girls in white dresses chattering excitedly on their way to their first communion. "The peace which to some degree may come in life was never . . . nearer . . . than in San Juan Capistrano," a visitor of 1889 had written. And it broods there still; peace, serenity, renewal, and the strength to once again return to the real world.

San Juan Capistrano's appeal did not go unnoticed by developers. Nearly every brochure for new housing tracts mentioned the city's heritage, its rural atmosphere, its lush orange groves, and its proximity to the ocean. Robert McCollum, a political activist of the 1970s, frequently pointed out that by building more and more homes developers were, in a sense, diminishing the very qualities that drew people to San Juan, qualities which were their chief selling points. The city councils of the seventies would address this issue, but the councils of the early sixties, while pledging to insure the rural character of the town, were at the same time hesitant about encroaching on the personal rights of the individual. One example of this was the fight over the Cañedo Adobe.

One of the most unique aspects of San Juan Capistrano was its number of adobe dwellings, some of them dating back possibly to 1794, and the rest to the 1840s. Most of the buildings had been renovated through the years and were in use as homes or businesses and one of these was an adobe which stood on the southeast corner of Ortega Highway and El Camino Real. Owned by the mission, it was sold in 1963 to Texas Oil Company (Texaco). The original walls were said to have been built by Isidro Aguilar, master mason of the Great Stone Church in the mission, sometime between 1797 and 1803. Others believe this adobe was one of the forty built by mission Indians in 1794. The building had been occupied in the 1850s and early 1860s by Salvador Canedo, the man attributed with bringing the germs of the black smallpox to San Juan which caused an epidemic of major proportions, killing, in the end, Salvador himself. Ironically, after the turn of the century, the adobe was used for wakes, a ceremony in which the body is placed in a coffin with candles at each end while mourners pray and chant over it prior to burial. Until it was purchased by the mission, the adobe was occupied by Aguilars and Paramos and in the 1840s briefly served as a store. Just before it was sold to Texaco it had been used by C. C. McCary as a real estate office.

Traditional dances were performed during the annual Swallows' Day Parade.
Courtesy of the San Juan Capistrano Historical Society

Monsignor Paul Martin
Courtesy of Richard Clinton

When the city council learned of the plans for the gas station they sought to save the adobe and were supported by many of their constituents. Les Remmers, representing the San Juan Capistrano Historical Society, which had been formed earlier that year, spoke before the council, saying, "we of the newly formed historical society ask each other what has happened to the present citizens and property owners of this city. Are we destroying something priceless — our heritage that cannot be replaced — to become another rubber stamp community?" The council asked the mission to help convince the Archdiocese of Los Angeles to save the building, but apparently it was too late. In July, the builder for Texaco came to the planning commission meeting and did nothing to ease the concerns of the community. He called the Cañedo Adobe an "atrocious example of architecture" and said it was no longer worth saving because it had electricity and plumbing. He also claimed the adobe building had been "moved onto the site" and had not been constructed there. He then offered to move it off. City officials, who believed

it was impossible to move an adobe structure, declined but hoped to convince him that the building should be made a part of the gas station office. City Attorney John Dawson then stepped in and told the council it had no right to make such a condition, that the only way to save the structure was to buy it. Struggling between upholding the rights of the property owner and preserving the unique character of the city, the council voted to allow the adobe to be destroyed. One councilman was quoted in the *Coastline Dispatch* as saying "owners have a legal right to do what they wish with their property. I don't think there is anyone in this room that would have it any other way." A pile of bricks and a marker today note the former location of the structure.

Two more landmarks were destroyed soon after the Cañedo Adobe. One was the Capistrano Hotel, sold in the spring of 1964 and torn down early in 1965. Built in 1920 by the Stoffel family, the hotel had thirty-four rooms and four apartments. It was later remodeled into ten apartments, its bottom floor containing a restaurant and bank. Before it was torn down, its owner, Dr. Konstantin Sparkuhl, opened it to the public for tours. Dr. Sparkuhl then built a wax museum on the site, but today the building is called the Capistrano Plaza and contains a number of shops.

The second landmark lost was the largest mansion in San Juan Capistrano, the Casa Grande. Built by Marcos Forster in 1882, it had served as a residence, a hotel, and the Los Rosas Restaurant. The owner, Lucana Forster McFadden, leased it to her goddaughter, Ventura Garcia Nieblas, and her husband Joe, in the late 1930s, and it was they who operated the Las Rosas Restaurant until Mrs. McFadden's death. The building was sold by the McFadden heirs in 1964 to a company owned by the Birtcher family of San Juan Capistrano. It was torn down and a Bank of America branch was built on the site and later became an office building.

In 1964, the American Institute of Architects, Orange County chapter, listed ten buildings worthy of consideration for the National Register of Historic Places. These included the Casa Grande, the Rios Adobe, the Avila Adobe,

The Labat House, dating back to the 1880s, still standing on Los Rios Street.
Courtesy of the San Juan Capistrano Historical Society

El Adobe Restaurant (made up of two adobes), the French Hotel (Oyharzabal's Garcia Adobe), the Pablo Pryor Adobe, Judge Richard Egan House, Blas Aguilar Adobe, Sievers' Canyon Adobe, and the Domingo Yorba Adobe.

The loss of old landmarks created a renewed interest in the history of the town. One person who did considerable research on Capistrano was attorney C. E. "Ted" Parker, who in April of 1966, informed the historical society that while doing title searches, he discovered that property owners in the downtown business district between El Camino Real, Yorba Street, Camino Capistrano, and Ortega Highway, did not have clear title to their land because it was once the village plaza. He told the group as a point of historical interest, but the ensuing furor could be heard all the way to Santa Ana. Parker's letter was run uncut on the front page of the *Coastline Dispatch*. Above the letter was another letter written by historical society president Gerald Gaffney, assuring everyone that the society had not put Parker up to it.

According to the attorney's research, when the U.S. government took over in 1848 and California became a state in 1850, the ownership of property in the Mexican pueblo known as San Juan Capistrano should have been surveyed and filed with the U.S. Land Commission. Because the commission did not act on and confirm the boundaries of the town or ownership of land, except for five tracts confirmed to the Catholic Church, the land was considered open. When the Homestead Acts were passed, the town was threatened because anyone could settle on any part of it (except for mission property) and file a homestead. Townsite Acts had been passed in 1864, 1865 and 1867 to protect unconfirmed towns like Capistrano, but according to these acts, only lots were safe; the streets and the town plaza were to remain public land (and not eligible for settlement). Ten years after the Townsite Acts were passed, San Juan Capistrano was surveyed and the ownership of its town lots was recorded. The plaza, which had existed up to this time, was now claimed by Jose Dolores Yorba, Mark Mendelson, Richard Egan, and Jonathan E. Bacon. The only way they could have legally occupied the area known as the plaza would have been if they had established their claims prior to 1864. This was not done, according to Parker, so the owners had no bonafide title to it, nor did the subsequent owners of those parcels. Nothing happened and the furor died down and the

*In 1926 the ruins of the north wing were taken out and construction
began on a replacement that would serve as the Mission School.
Courtesy of the San Juan Capistrano Mission Archives*

information was accepted as a quirk of history, nothing more. When city officials began to consider the possible construction of a downtown plaza in 1975, Parker sent them a letter noting the boundaries of the original plaza. Today the site of the original plaza is owned by the Community Redevelopment Agency and is once again public property.

Another structure was lost in late 1965, but no one mourned its passing. It was a wooden shed, located on the north side of Ortega Highway about a mile and a half from the center of town. It wasn't an old building, but some people felt a twinge of nostalgia toward it — it reminded them of the Roaring Twenties and when it went, it went with style. It was a still.

"Moonshiner Arrested in Capo — Revenoors [sic] Destroy Corn Still" said the headline in the *Santa Ana Register* on August 6, 1965. "Orange County Sheriff's deputies and U. S. Treasury department agents moved into upper Capistrano

Valley early today to smash what they called an illegal corn liquor operation," reported the newspaper. One deputy said he'd known about the moonshine for six months, but couldn't trace it. The culprit, who turned out to be the local Santa Fe agent, admitted he had made it, but said he was "only experimenting, not selling." Treasury agents said information leading to the arrest had been gathered by agents "making buys mostly." The agents were surprised to find two stills in one building.

"Already inoperative when agents moved in was an 800-gallon copper still at one time capable of producing 80 gallons of the clear corn liquor at one boiling, the agent said. Found in operating condition was the 110-gallon still capable of producing from 10 to 12 gallons per run. Also found in the building were 30 one-gallon bottles filled with liquor and six 55-gallon barrels of corn mash. A treasury agent said the still was heated by burning old lumber and logs."

The moonshiner and an assistant went to court

166

the following February, and were convicted despite a defense which included testimony by a 92-year-old father of twenty-six who claimed he was the moonshiner.

"The Ozark-born grandfather, who said he had been distilling moonshine for 80 years, insisted it was he who had the still installed," reported the Register on February 19. The grandfather said it had been built for him by a friend who fled to the hills of Kentucky.

One other landmark was lost in the late sixties. This building was not old or picturesque, but its passing was symbolic of the changes that had taken place in San Juan Capistrano in thirty years. It was the old Blue Goose packing house. The building burned down in 1969, creating a blaze that could be seen for miles. It burned all night, for a time threatening other historic buildings in the downtown area, and when morning came nothing was left but the basement. Many people lined the streets the night it burned, people who had packed oranges in wooden crates, who had driven the crates into town from the fields, who had danced until midnight on the smooth floor on weekends. The death of the packing house was symbolic of the death of a way of life longtime residents of San Juan had known. Gone were the barbecues under the sycamores where everybody knew everyone else. Gone were the freshmen from old Capo High who climbed the hill on the west side of the valley, armed with toothbrushes to clean the old concrete "C." Gone was the tiny downtown area where a six-year-old could wander through the mission and browse in the stores, stopping to greet each shopkeeper and waving to friends in the occasional cars that passed. San Juan had grown up, it had the responsibilities of a mature city. It was, as Councilman Jim Thorpe had characterized it in 1970, "a little city with big city problems."

In 1969, the city was inundated by floods which washed away two bridges and several roads, made homes near the creek beds unlivable, and severely strained the city budget. Repairs were made and finances remained intact and the city sailed through the crisis. Expenditures for public works projects were usually not too heavily questioned. But in the early seventies, the council decided the city was ready for its own police department, and this time

people got out microscopes to examine the city budget. After a furor which lasted well over a year and a controversy which tore the community in two, the idea was abandoned and the city continued its contract with the county sheriff. The crisis passed.

After the police controversy, people began to assess the type of city San Juan had become. By 1970, it was a boom town; new construction was evident in most sections of the city. Plans poured into City Hall so fast that an assistant planner had to be hired. Planning Commission and City Council meetings lasted well past midnight. The city no longer had tourism as its only economic base. A small industrial park had been built in the southern part of the city, with industries locating in other parts of the city as well; new shopping centers were going up. And though most people still worked outside the city limits, they did much of their shopping locally. San Juan was indeed a city.

In the 1970s, many began to lament the loss of the small town. Newcomers as well as oldtimers looked around them and asked if it was too late to bring back the San Juan Capistrano of yesterday. If it was, then retain the flavor of yesterday, the rural character, the village atmosphere. Do something now, they said, before it all disappeared.

Some people argued that it was too late for rural flavor, that growth was inevitable, that San Juan Capistrano was a city, and urbanization and farming were incompatible. The course had been set, they said, and those who tried to alter it were not only interfering with personal rights, but were deluding themselves. Others said it was not too late, that the course could be altered for the sake of community quality. If individual rights got in the way, they would have to be adjusted for the sake of the public good.

In the election of 1974, the community divided itself into two camps — those who believed that individual rights took precedence and those who believed the public good should come first. There were even fights over definitions of "individual rights" and "public good." When it was over three councilmen had been elected who had run on a platform of limiting growth, retaining the rural character of the city, and preserving the hillsides. Once in office they began charting the new course, one which included the preparation of a new General

Plan for future development which projected an ultimate population of forty-two thousand residents for the city, half as many as the old plan had called for. Proponents called it a workable solution and set about seeing that implementing ordinances would insure the development of the city according to the new plan. Opponents shook their heads and said it would not only devaluate property and render it undevelopable, but would eventually bankrupt the citizenry.

Spokesmen on both sides were eloquent, both viewpoints had merit, and both sides admitted that the dialogue was healthy. They also agreed that San Juan Capistrano was a unique community and had much to preserve.

As the city's bicentennial neared, citizens were very much aware of their heritage. Bicycle trail markers and stoplight backs were embellished with swallows and mission bells. The historical society had over five hundred members and actively campaigned to build a museum to preserve reminders of the community's past. Walking tours, formally begun in 1974 by Mary Jane Forster, and informally started even earlier by Doris Drummond, educated the public about the city's historic structures. The Fiesta de Las Golondrinas Association annually put on a parade and a week of activities to celebrate the return of the swallows, an event which drew thousands each year. The Architectural Board of Review, a committee appointed by the City Council, continued to encourage builders of homes and businesses to use Spanish architectural styles.

Heritage was a popular topic as San Juan Capistrano approached its two hundredth birthday. But it would face its most difficult challenge in the 1980s and the face of the downtown would once again be the issue.

Here is an artists view of downtown in the 1890s. The painting was on the cover of the bicentennial calendar developed by the Chamber of Commerce. Courtesy of the San Juan Capistrano Historical Society

Chapter 9

Beginning the Next Two Hundred Years
1976 – 1990

In 1976, America drenched itself in a wave of nostalgia as its two hundredth anniversary approached. Bicentennial specials dominated television listings and the liberty bell popped up on everything from pencils to car license plates. In Orange County, bicentennial fever was just as strong, but the economy was not. The war in Vietnam had ended in 1970, plunging the aerospace industry into a decline, and the county's spiraling growth rate suddenly slowed to a crawl as a period of recession and inflation set in.

San Juan Capistrano, which had purposely slowed growth in its community through the adoption of a new general plan, was less affected by the change of events than other areas. But it was more affected by the bicentennial, primarily because it had one of its own to celebrate — the two hundredth anniversary of the founding of the mission. The town celebration would come in November, but the first event to create an interest in the past occurred in January. It was the visit of the Freedom Train.

The Freedom Train, which carried such Americana as the original Golden Spike and Wilt Chamberlain's basketball shoe, pulled into Orange County on January 9, stopping first in Anaheim. Its second stop on its way south was San Juan Capistrano and people lined up for hours to view the memorabilia. The train was located on the double track adjacent to Los Rios Street and the entire downtown had to be closed to traffic to accommodate the five-block-long line.

Taking advantage of the event, community groups set up booths in the downtown, provided entertainment for the visitors in line, and sold hundreds of hot dogs and soft drinks. When the train pulled out, it left a residue of pride and a renewed interest in the past, something the city of San Juan Capistrano took advantage of.

The new General Plan, adopted in December of 1974, had called for the formation of a Cultural Heritage Commission to oversee the identification and preservation of historic structures in the community. The first commission was appointed in 1975 and the first official inventory of historic structures was adopted by the City Council in 1976. Buildings on this list included such well-known structures as Mission San Juan Capistrano, the Rios Adobe, and the Montanez Adobe. It also contained lesser-known buildings like the English House and the Hot Springs Dance Hall, buildings that had deteriorated and were in the path of downtown development.

The ordinance required that the buildings be preserved, either by restoring them, rehabilitating them for some other adaptive reuse, or, as a last resort, by moving them. The Cultural Heritage Commission had the right to deny demolition and to review any structural or cosmetic alterations to the buildings or the site. The owner had the right to appeal decisions the Commission made to the City Council.

At the time of adoption, this was one of the most far-reaching preservation ordinances in the state. Many cities had architectural controls; none had a clause that prohibited demolition.

The first challenge to the preservation ordinance came from the owner of the Richard Egan House, who did not want it listed on the

Orange County Supervisor Tom Riley, left, helps Mayor Doug Nash dedicate a plaque in honor of the Nation's Bicentennial in 1976.
Courtesy of the San Juan Capistrano Historical Society

based developer Robert Maurer built his Villages of the Mission on Ortega Highway, three historic structures were in the path of development. The Harrison House and the Parra Adobe, today the home of the Capistrano Indian Council, were donated to the city, and the Errecarte House was refurbished and sold, remaining at the entrance to the tract as a historic reminder of the area's agricultural history.

The area of town drawing the most interest was that known as Los Rios.

Los Rios, a forty-acre planning area set aside for special treatment, had contained residential units since 1794. Three of them — the Rios, Montanez, and Silvas Adobes — were still standing. The majority of the other dwelling units were of board and batten con-

inventory for philosophical reasons. The house, which had both architectural and historical significance to the community, remained on the list. The Council refused to remove it.

Another challenge came when the Hot Springs Dance Hall, once located across from the west side of the mission, was scheduled for demolition. The owner's permit was denied, but since the building had not been built on the site, but had been moved there, a compromise was reached. The building was donated to the city and was relocated at a cost of five thousand dollars to the rear of the City Hall property. It was rehabilitated as a Senior Center and instead of being a duplex as it was in its downtown location, it once again became a community building.

The English House, also in the path of development, was also, earmarked for demolition. Located north of Durenberger's Antiques, the building was once a residence and had for a time been used as a restaurant. The owner was required to give the house away. After advertising, resident Bill Hardy came forward and was determined by the city to have the best location. Other applicants wanted to move the house out of town. Hardy moved it to Ramos Street where there were similar board and batten residences, and it was refurbished for use as a home.

Not all houses could be moved. When Tustin-

Father Paul Martin is seen here in a 1976 procession through Serra Chapel during the 200th Anniversary of the founding of the mission. Behind him is Bishop Johnson and Cardinal Manning.
Courtesy of the San Juan Capistrano Historical Society

Linda Dunn and William Reid, Jr., take bows after a performance of Pro Patria, an historic play written by Don Meadows. The production was part of San Juan's bicentennial celebration and took place in front of Oyharzabal barn.
Courtesy of the San Juan Capistrano Historical Society

in the Los Rios area.

The General Plan itself was the product of years of study. Based on the Citizens Policy Plan, a set of goals developed by more than one hundred people in 1973, the General Plan was developed with the assistance of the planning firm of Haworth and Anderson. It envisioned a population of forty-two thousand at build-out living in a balanced community with emphasis on historic character, a rural atmosphere, and abundant open space. The General Plan, with thirteen separate elements, and the accompanying growth control ordinance, which allowed 350 units to be built a year, provided an outline for the future.

struction and had been built at the turn of the century. A Pasadena planning firm, the Arroyo Group, was hired to prepare a master plan for the area, using the charette system, a planning tool that used a high degree of citizen involvement. After several years of study and fine-tuning, a plan was adopted which generally kept it a neighborhood where owner-occupied businesses could stand next to residential uses. The goal was to retain the character of the community with narrow streets, unpaved shoulders, and wooden structures. The plan, when adopted, was overseen by the Los Rios Review Committee, a group of owners and residents

The Egan House in 1990 looks much as it did one hundred years ago.
Courtesy of the San Juan Capistrano Historical Society

171

Downtown scene in the 1970s of San Juan Capistrano.
Courtesy of the San Juan Capistrano Historical Society

city set up an agriculture preservation fund which was fed by a special development fee. This money could be used for fencing, well problems, and other needs upon application by the farmer to the city.

Opponents of the plan, who considered this an excessive restriction on the property owner's rights, asked that an advisory vote be placed on the ballot. It was and in 1976 the community voted by a wide majority to retain agriculture in this manner. Owners, the majority of whom were still farming, chose not to challenge the zoning in the courts.

The decade of the 1970s was one of review and redefinition. Communities surrounding the city were rapidly developing, creating traffic problems that were spilling over into San Juan Capistrano. The mission had embarked on a vigorous marketing program, and had opened an off-site visitor's center to handle the details. Downtown parking, always a problem, was getting worse. Studies showed that while the

Although there were challenges to the plan, the only major loss was to Glendale Federal Development Company, which challenged it in court on the basis that their land-use densities had been higher in the old plan and their land values were therefore affected. The court upheld Glendale Federal's claim and exempted them from the city's growth control ordinance. In the compromise settlement, originally approved densities were reduced, however, and the city was able to obtain 850 acres of permanent open space over major ridgelines above the project. Their developments, constructed on the hills above the San Juan Hills golf course, changed the visual character of the community.

One of the more controversial components of the General Plan was the preservation of agriculture. Property bounded by Alipaz, Del Avion, and Del Obispo found itself zoned for permanent agriculture, as did several properties north of the city. The land was all under cultivation at the time and had excellent soil. To assist farmers, the

Here is an aerial view of the 40-acre Los Rios area set aside for special study. Today, portions of it are listed on the National Register of Historic Places. Courtesy of the San Juan Capistrano Historical Society

This is a view of eastern valley looking southwest from the hilltop equestrian trail.
Courtesy of the San Juan Capistrano Historical Society

downtown was active, downtown businesses were not doing the volume that they should.

Solutions were available, but they were long-range and costly. San Juan Capistrano was different. It was the oldest settlement in Orange County, its heritage and goals were unique, and its future would take careful planning.

To help the city with its decisions, consultants were hired to draw a plan for the downtown. One of a series of such plans that would be commissioned over the years, this plan called for narrowing Camino Capistrano by widening sidewalks, installing landscaped areas, and using pavers. One version called for closing off Camino Capistrano; another called for making the two town center streets one-way. Hearings were held, but no one could agree. The plan was shelved.

One recommendation in the plan, however, was to upgrade the parking lot east of the Capistrano Depot. A dirt lot with broken pavement and abandoned vehicles, the area contained a series of owners who couldn't agree on what to

do. The city acquired rights to the property, obtained a grant for the construction of multi-modal terminal, and built a parking lot and outdoor waiting area for people using such modes of transportation as cars, buses, and bicycles. The lot was used for limited-term parking and the lot north of the depot was

Hot Springs Dance Hall, refurbished as a Senior Center, opened in 1978.
Courtesy of the San Juan Capistrano Historical Society

The dedication of Multimodal Terminal in 1983 had participants from Caltrans, Trailways, and Amtrak present.
Courtesy of the San Juan Capistrano Historical Society

again. Some uses had to be re-evaluated.

As the 1970s came to a close it became obvious that one of the services that was not keeping up with growth was the public library. A number of storefront buildings had housed the library for over fifty years, but that choice was no longer acceptable. The town needed its own library building.

To make it happen sooner, the city leased a site at the corner of Acjachema and El Camino Real from the Capistrano Unified School District, and offered it to the county. To insure architectural control, the city offered to pay all architectural fees and any costs above the amount of funding usually provided by used for Amtrak commuters.

The Capistrano Depot, constructed during 1894, had not been in official use as a train station since Santa Fe ended its passenger service in the 1950s. Amtrak, which started in 1971, served the community only as a flag stop, ending service in 1972. Through community pressure, San Juan Capistrano was re-added as an Amtrak stop in 1974 and has continued to be a regular stop along the Lossan Corridor with sixteen trains a day and more planned.

From 1966 to 1974, the depot was boarded up and served only as a curiosity. In September of 1974, construction began to renovate the structure for a new use — a restaurant. It was completed in May of 1975 by Peter and James Tyson, who leased the building from the Santa Fe Land and Improvement Company. The renovation was done at a cost of $650,000, which included moving old railroad cars in for additional space, developing the site, and buying the furnishings. The Tysons sold their interest to the Community Redevelopment Agency in the late eighties and the building has been refurbished for continued use as a restaurant.

But not all buildings could be upgraded for continued use. The community was starting to grow

Mariachis play for the dedication of the Multimodal Terminal in 1983.
Courtesy of the San Juan Capistrano Historical Society

The award-winning library by Michael Graves opened amid controversy in 1983.
Courtesy of Mark Gibson

the county for construction of its branch libraries. The Board of Supervisors agreed and the process began.

The need to make the building special was underscored, not only by its proximity to the mission, but also by the fact that it would be the first public building the city had ever constructed. It was decided that a design competition should be held and in the summer of 1980, advertisements were placed in all the major architectural magazines and newsletters. The response was overwhelming. At the deadline, there were forty completed applications and the names of the firms were among the most prominent in the world.

A committee of citizens was selected to review the design statements, examples of work, and the overall philosophies of the candidates. After narrowing the choices to five, interviews were held and three finalists chosen — Moore, Ruble, Yudell of Los Angeles; Robert A. M. Stern of New York; and Michael Graves of Princeton. The finalists submitted models of their proposals and the committee, on a split vote, recommended the Graves design.

One committee member was later quoted as saying, "The Graves design terrified. It was bold,

untraditional, exotic. Yet the ties to history were readily apparent. It was not San Juan Capistrano

Councilman Ken Friess, right, disburses "fix up" grants to residents of Los Rios Street. On hand to witness the historic moment were Juanita Rios Foy, matriarch of San Juan Capistrano, Maria Browne, and Steve Rios.
Courtesy of the San Juan Capistrano Historical Society

San Juan Capistrano City Council has been the same for twelve years. Shown in western wear for annual Fiesta de las Golondrinas are, from left, Ken Friess, Gary Hausdorfer, Larry Buchheim, Tony Bland, and Phil Schwartze.
Courtesy of Tom Baker

town, after the mission. Tourists came from all over the world to see it, yet locally it was still either loved or hated, and the controversy rages even today.

Two groups formed to support the library. The first was Friends of the Library, which had existed previously, and primarily supported the activities of the library, itself. The Friends built a very successful bookstore to provide funds for their ongoing activities. The second was a new group, Libros y Artes. This group, headed by well-known antiquarian Gep Durenberger, was a cultural arm of the city, using the Sala, or community room, of the library for its exhibits. The group soon outgrew its exhibit space and, through the assistance of the city, purchased a building across

architecture. But it exuded a powerful influence and made people think about architecture. It was not a miniature mission. It would become a landmark in its own right."

The recommendation was submitted to the City Council and the ensuing controversy over the design raged for several months. People loved it or hated it. There was no in-between. The Council, torn with the need to please constituents, but unwilling to nullify the work of the committee, invited Graves to make a public presentation to explain his symbolism. He did. Partially succumbing to the charisma of the man and his imagery, and partially sensing the importance of the decision for the future, they voted unanimously for his design.

The library was completed in 1983, set circulation records for the library system, and became the most photographed building in

Serving as the city hall for over twenty years was a building at the end of Paseo Adelanto designed to be a Public Works facility.
Courtesy of Mark Gibson

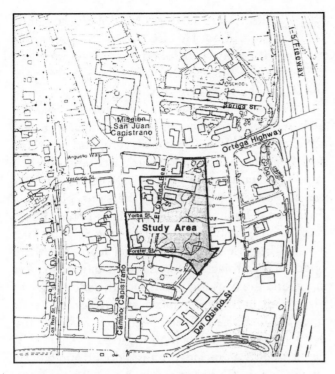

The shaded area shows the vicinity of significant archeological finds during 1989 in the downtown. Courtesy of the San Juan Capistrano Historical Society

Camino Capistrano which is now the Decorative Arts Center.

North of the library stood the remaining buildings of the old high school. Used over the years for various purposes, and currently used for adult education and as a continuation high school, the buildings gained their own prominence in the community. The Capistrano Unified School District built several high schools after Capistrano Union High School closed and even gave one of them a similar name, but none of the schools were ever built within the city limits. Marco Forster Junior High was built in the community, as were Del Obispo and Ambuehl elementary schools, but the only high schools in the city were private — St. Margaret's and Capistrano Valley Christian.

Yet the old high school site was about to get a new purpose. The city announced in the late eighties that the old high school would become the site of the new civic center. Existing buildings, dating from 1939, would be retained, and new buildings constructed on vacant portions of the property. The civic center is currently being master-planned.

The old City Hall, which in 1970 was dedicated as a public works facility, will finally become what it was intended to be. For twenty years it served as a "temporary city hall" and was remodeled and enlarged over the years until it outgrew its site. Spruced up with the assistance of Danielson Design Group, the old "butler building" took on a more sophisticated look in 1985, but it couldn't be expanded any further. The new civic center is slated for design and construction in the early 1990s.

While the future of the old high school buildings seem secure, the fate of the downtown was unsettled. In 1987, yet another downtown study was completed which called for Ortega Highway to be relocated from Del Obispo to Camino Capistrano, for El Camino Real to become a walkway between Forster and the new Ortega Highway, and for several new buildings to be constructed in vacant spaces on both sides of El Camino Real. San Diego-based developer Oliver McMillan submitted the approved proposal and became the official developer for what was called the Historic Town Center. Over the years the Community Redevelopment Agency had been methodically buying property in the block bounded by Ortega Highway, Camino Capistrano, Forster Street and on both sides of El Camino Real. The purpose was to get these properties under single ownership so that they could be master-planned and developed as a unit, rather than as unrelated pieces. Suggested uses were restaurants and shops. But one

Archeological find in the Great Stone Church. Former grave site of two padres. Courtesy of the San Juan Capistrano Historical Society

Franciscan Plaza, completed in 1990, was built on site of earlier buildings constructed in 1973. Despite ground disturbances through the past one hundred years, foundations of early adobes were found intact during construction.
Courtesy of Mark Gibson

of the components of the plan was to construct a hotel where the Mendelson Inn had once stood.

Although no formal plans were submitted for a hotel, people began to take sides over the size, style, and even the necessity for a hotel in the downtown. One plan, submitted by the Friends of Historic San Juan, a new political action preservation group, suggested that replicas of original adobe structures should be built, to bring back the character of the community as it was in the mid-nineteenth century. Another suggestion was that the Mendelson Inn should be rebuilt on its original site, along with the Las Rosas and some of the other buildings that had stood at the turn of the century. Yet another suggestion was to leave the spaces vacant, leaving the downtown unchanged.

While rhetoric flew, the Community Redevelopment Agency hired LSA Associates to conduct a formal archaeological study of the vacant spaces to determine what, if anything, was left of the adobes and other later structures that had once occupied the site. Focus then changed to the opposite side of the downtown, to the real historic town center where original adobes were still standing and in use. A development project had been submitted which once again appeared to divide the community. It was the construction of a movie theater.

Laguna Beach developer Paul Farber had quietly purchased the Franciscan Plaza, a series of

shops built in 1973 at the corner of Verdugo and Camino Capistrano. He also owned the properties to the west which included a small apartment building and a brick and lumber storage yard (once the site of the Blue Goose packing house).

Farber's approved plans called for the construction of a new multi-story Franciscan Plaza, a theater where the apartments were, and a parking structure where the storage yard once was, the two latter structures facing Verdugo Street. The theater was to be located at precisely the same place that Fred Cason began showing movies in the 1920s, prior to building his theater where the Trading Post is today. But Friends of Historic San Juan and others opposed the projects because the buildings were too large, and the uses too intense for the site. The city responded by ordering more archaeological work since the plans had already been approved and the developments were moving forward.

Discoveries included more adobe foundations along Camino Capistrano, which would have been the remains of two adobes listed in the 1936 WPA report, *Adobes of Orange County*, and may have at one time been attached to the Avila Adobe, and some other structural remains in the parking structure area. The finds were documented and mitigated and the projects were built.

Additional archaeological work was underway across town, in what had once been Mission Tract No. 5, the former Stroschein property. Remains of an adobe wall, which had once enclosed a mission-period crop growing area, was found where a Sizzler Restaurant was being built. Plans shifted the building

The theater dates from 1989 on Verdugo Street.
Courtesy of Mark Gibson

The 1987 El Viaje de Portolá gathers on Camino Capistrano en route for its blessing at the mission. The annual event commemorates Portolá's expedition through California.
Courtesy of Mike Darnold

slightly and the wall was set aside for preservation. The rest of the tract, which was across the street between Del Obispo and the freeway where a drive-in theater had stood for the past twenty years, did not reveal any further evidence of the wall. A shopping center was built on that site and archaeological work was done prior to construction.

The price tag for community archeology was climbing, and had passed $300,000. While developers paid for some of the archaeological work, the city and the Community Redevelopment Agency paid for most. The richest area for archaeological finds was the downtown, and most of the downtown property south of the mission was now owned by the public. Results of the archaeological studies on El Camino Real began to come in. The finds were extremely significant, with foundations of several adobe buildings still intact after two hundred years. Any development in the area would have to be reevaluated.

"The original plans we had for the downtown are simply not going to fly," said Councilman Ken Friess in an interview with *Los Angeles Times* newspaper reporter Wendy Paulson in October

1989. "It is not possible to do the amount of development we hoped to do because we have a lot of archaeological treasures down there."

Because of the sensitivity and the long-range effects of the archaeological work in the downtown area, the city hired the well-known archaeological firm of Greenwood and Associates to become staff consultants on all public archeology. They also ordered further studies of the downtown area to determine the extent and significance of the finds and to allow the consultant to make recommendations on which areas should be preserved and which could be built upon. Studies are still underway.

Archaeological treasures were not just confined to the public portions of the downtown. A few blocks away at Mission San Juan Capistrano significant work was also being done, work that was sanctioned by the Diocese of Orange and led by Father Paul Martin.

Father Martin, who had been assistant pastor at the mission from 1961 to 1970, was appointed pastor in 1978. He brought with him a love of history, which found ample outlets in his stewardship

The Albert Pryor House before restoration as O'Neill Museum is pictured here. It was located behind the El Adobe Restaurant parking lot, near the railroad tracks. Courtesy of the San Juan Capistrano Historical Society

indicated that his approach was indeed not just in the field of archeology, but there would be historians, and artists and there would be people of varying disciplines brought together under one banner, I saw that truly this was the one thing I was personally looking for."

The archaeological research project was launched, sponsored by Chapman College, with assistance at various times from the University of California, Irvine, and Rancho Santiago College, Santa Ana. As it continued, it became apparent that a need existed for a museum of professional caliber where the artifacts being uncovered could be displayed and catalogued. A plan was presented to Father Martin, sanctioned by the Diocese of Orange, and begun with the help of donations. The first museum

of the mission. Though trained in theology and philosophy, he was anxious to do some field work at the mission, similar to what was being done in other missions. In 1979, he got that opportunity when Professor Nicholas Magalousis knocked on his door.

"I have always had a personal awareness that sometimes when we work in isolation in our particular field and we don't interrelate with one another in our varying disciplines, we can perhaps not receive the richness of decisions and interpretations we other wise could," said Father Martin, in "Ten Years of Interdisciplinary Studies at Mission San Juan Capistrano" printed in the *Proceedings of the Conference of Orange County History, 1988.* "When Professor Magalousis

The Pryor House was moved across Santa Fe tracks to its new home on Los Rios Street. Courtesy of the San Juan Capistrano Historical Society

room was established in 1980 and was dedicated to local Native Americans. That same year an extensive program of cataloguing began, and the second museum room was completed with funds acquired from Viaje de Portola, the Ahmanson Foundation, James Irvine Foundation, O'Neill-Avery Foundation,

Members of the O'Neill family gather around San Juan Capistrano Historical Society President Anne Schauwecker, third from right, in 1978 to view plans for the restoration of the Pryor house, thanks to their $60,000 donation. From left are Jerome Moiso, Alice Avery, Richard O'Neill, Tony Moiso, and Douglas Avery.
Courtesy of the San Juan Capistrano Historical Society

The corner of Los Rios and River Streets, future sight of the O'Neill Museum. Carmen, Eugenia Oyharzabal and Anne Schauwecker.
Courtesy of the San Juan Capistrano Historical Society

Mission San Juan Capistrano, and Friends of the Museum. The museum soon grew to eight rooms with an outdoor "living history" area where activities common to various periods of time are conducted by volunteers in appropriate costumes. Por-

O'Neill Museum, formerly the Pryor House, opened in 1978. It took two years to prepare the site, restore the building, and arrange fencing.
Courtesy of Mike Darnold

tions of the grounds were also included as museum exhibits, particularly the metalworking furnaces which were discovered during the digs and have been found to be the oldest in California.

Since education was the primary motive for exploring the mission grounds, a docent program was established in 1980 to share with the public the discoveries being made in the mission grounds. By charging a modest fee for tours, the docents have contributed over $10,000 to the mission projects and have acquainted thousands of visitors with the mission's history and significance. In addition, an outreach program has also been developed to take the mission right into school classrooms.

The most ambitious project during the decade was the construction of a new parish church. Built along the lines of the original Great Stone Church, but increased in size to meet parish needs, St. John's Church was constructed at the north end of the

*This corner destined to become home of O'Neill Museum was owned
by Oyharzabal family.
Courtesy of the San Juan Capistrano Historical Society*

The church was officially dedicated in 1987.

Looking back over the past ten years, Father Martin credits the success of the mission's various programs to many dedicated parishioners. But the cultural resource program's success is credited to Magalousis, who was able to take moments of time and make them into a historic continuum. His view, as was Father Martin's, was that the mission was not something from the past, but was a place that had a viable present and future. Yet the future was of concern to both, particularly after the earthquake of October 1987, when nearby Mission San Gabriel

mission property on Acjachema Street. Designed by architect John Bartlett, the interior of the church was researched and designed by art historian Norman Neuerberg, who personally painted many of the wall designs. The bells in the belltower were a gift of the Birtcher family of San Juan Capistrano.

*Clint Eastwood emerges from a trailer on the set of
Heartbreak Ridge, a portion of which was filmed in San Juan
Capistrano in 1986. Trailers were set up in El Peon's parking
lot for easy access to the Swallow Inn, one of the sets.
Courtesy of Mike Darnold*

*David Belardes, Tribal Chairman of the Juaneño Band
of Mission Indians, confers with Rita Avila,
a member of an old San Juan family.
Courtesy of Mike Darnold*

was so severely damaged that it had to be closed.

Again, using the interdisciplinary approach, a team of experts were gathered to evaluate the structural integrity of the mission buildings, particularly the ruins. To help in this diagnostic, Ms. Kalliope Theocharidou, a specialist in Byzantine structures, was flown in from Greece to make detailed recommendations. In an interview in the

Preparing steaks at a 1987 Heritage Barbeque are, from left, Tony Forster, Steve Julian, Mike Darnold, and Pat Forster. Courtesy of Mike Darnold

Los Angeles Times, Theocharidou commented that although she had studied photographs of the mission before she arrived, the problem was much worse

Councilman Larry Buchheim and wife, Pat, enjoy the Heritage Barbeque in 1987. Courtesy of Mike Darnold

than she had expected. Different types of stones of "poor quality" had been used over the years, and they were now deteriorating.

After examining virtually every stone, recommendations will be made on how to chemically alter them to make them stronger. Thin steel rods will then be used to bind roofs to walls and walls to floors, without anyone knowing they are there.

The project is expected to take ten years and

several million dollars. Most of the funds will be raised through private donations. Theocharidou, addressing an audience of local citizens in August of 1989, on the night the stabilization project was officially introduced to the public, characterized the mission as "California's Acropolis," and well worth the effort required to preserve it.

Echoing her thoughts, Nicholas Magalousis called the mission a "world class historical site," and said the work would involve researchers, contractors,

Marlene Draper interviews Paul Arbiso, community patriarch, at the Heritage Barbeque in 1987. The barbeque honors members of San Juan's oldest families. Courtesy of Mike Darnold

Marilyn Thorpe, one of the Historical Society's Walking Tour Guide, examining the Tour Guide map in front of the former El Peon Center.
Courtesy of the San Juan Capistrano Historical Society

and the business community. "It appears this will be one of the largest preservation projects in the state of California," he said.

While the philosophy of mission officials has been to stabilize rather than restore or reconstruct, the city's philosophy has been different, evaluating each situation on a case by case basis. In March of 1990, Paul Farber, owner of the Avila Adobe announced that he would restore the building back to its earliest known appearance and would use it as a restaurant. On the opposite side of the original town plaza, the Community Redevelopment Agency announced it would restore the Blas Aguilar Adobe and use it for community education programs. With new sensitivity toward downtown discoveries, both in and out of the mission, and with new emphasis on structural stabilization of historic buildings, both by choice and because of new state laws, the city's preservation program once again became the center of attention.

But preservation in San Juan Capistrano has not always focused only on the past. It has also looked to the future. In 1986, the San Juan Capistrano Historical Society launched an ambitious project to carry community history into every

fourth grade classroom in the Capistrano Unified School District. With costumed docents, a community history video, a trunk full of artifacts, and well-trained volunteers, the school docent program was launched which annually reaches nearly two thousand youngsters. The teachers often follow up with a downtown walking tour conducted by trained volunteer guides who have been interpreting the downtown for visitors for two decades. These programs, coupled with a scholarship, oral history, and adult lecture series, and the operation of the O'Neill Museum, which opened in 1978 through the generosity of the O'Neill family, the historical society continues to provide a valuable service to the community.

Yet historic preservation is only a part of what makes San Juan Capistrano unique. Open space, much of it in its natural state, is another and this became an issue in 1990 when a grass roots organization formed to save 140 acres of open space for recreational uses. Called the Committee to Save Open Space, it was headed by Marlene Draper and proposed to the voters of the city a ballot measure which would authorize the sale of $21 million in bonds to purchase 20 acres of the Kinoshita Ranch near Alipaz and Del Avion and 120 acres of land adjacent to the Bathgate Ranch at the northernmost boundary of the city. After an intense and well-organized campaign, the voters went to the polls on April 10, and when the votes were counted the measure had won by 71 percent of the vote. Under California law, it had needed a two-thirds majority in order to pass since it was a measure which would increase property taxes. Once again the community showed that it was in favor of preservation, despite the price tag. "San Juan has a long history of caring about values more than economics," said Mayor Gary Hausdorfer, in an interview in the *Los Angeles Times* in November of 1989. "This is open space that cannot be replaced."

San Juan Capistrano today is a place that is different from other cities in Orange County and is proud of those differences. Yet, in its quest for a quality lifestyle, the city has not neglected basic services. Since incorporation, the city has contracted with the Orange County Sheriffs Department for police protection, an

El Adobe Folkorico Dancers march in the 1989 Fiesta de las Golondrinas Parade.
Courtesy of Mike Darnold

arrangement that has been more economical than starting a local police department. The arrangement has also been satisfactory in that services can be tailored to the needs of the community. In past years, there has been a "foot patrol" in the downtown during the summer months when tourism is heaviest and "creek patrols" on horseback when special needs arise.

The city has also continued to contract with the Orange County Fire Department for fire suppression and paramedic services. With a population estimated at twenty-eight thousand, the city is served by one station located within the community, with back-up stations on its borders. Today's fire department has a full-time, 24-hour staff which is supplemented by a county-wide staff of six hundred full time and volunteer personnel. The volunteers, which train weekly, are particularly valuable during dry months when numerous brush fires threaten thousands of acres in the nearby Cleveland National Forest. The worst to date has been the Stewart Fire which blackened seventy thousand acres in 1958 and had two thousand firefighters on the scene. No other brush fires to date have been as destructive.

With an emphasis on rural character, the community has developed several miles of equestrian/hiking trails, has chosen not to line its creekbeds with concrete, and has worked out

agreements with some neighbors not to build on top of ridgelines. It is a place where commercial development, much of which has been in the

Children wear traditional Hispanic costumes during the Fiesta de las Golondrinas parade in 1989.
Courtesy of Mike Darnold

Children watch a face painter apply her skills during the 1988 Heritage Festival community picnic.
Courtesy of Mike Darnold

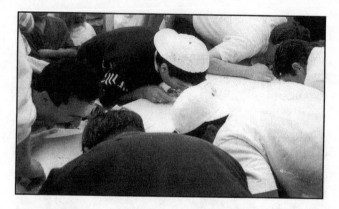

The pie-eating contest was a favorite event at the 1988 Heritage Festival.
Courtesy of Mike Darnold

Bill Luke enjoys the thrill of victory at the 1988 Heritage Festival pie-eating contest.
Courtesy of Mike Darnold

planning stages for years, has finally been constructed on the periphery of the downtown, where road improvements such as bridge widening and freeway ramps, long overdue, are finally going to bid, and where water conservation is promoted and encouraged. It is a place where you can still see hillsides full of wildflowers in the spring, horsemen riding out from one of several commercial stables along the riverbeds, and where trees and swallows have laws that protect them.

At the center of the town is the mission, whose social, economic, and cultural influence through two centuries is undeniable. Its political influence has been more subtle and is harder to assess. Today's mission, with its cultivated gardens and natural grace, stands like a citadel in the midst of change. It is an original in a field of imitations; it has earned the right to remain, if it chooses, aloof and untouched by the crises and controversies of the town that surrounds it. It is, today, a sanctuary, a step into the past where a person can find peace and tranquility and the comfort of permanence in a time when very little stays the same.

There is a garden behind the bells where water in a stone fountain moves only with the whisper of the wind. If you listen on a crisp winter morning you can almost hear the chanting of Indians at their morning prayers. If you stare into the water you can see back two hundred years to the little cavalcade, surrounded by curious Indians, who pounded a wooden cross into the hard earth to found Mission San Juan Capistrano while a continent away, a young country struggled for survival, its young men staining the earth with blood in pursuit of liberty. Their symbol was the liberty bell which still stands today, more than two hundred years later. San Juan Capistrano's symbol is a row of mission bells and two hundred years from now, they'll still be there.

Lauranne Collins and Cheryl Bower from Seaside Stompers clog during 1988 Heritage Festival.
Courtesy of the San Juan Capistrano Historical Society

Pat Huber and Rita Avila sell ice cream for the San Juan Historical Society during the
1988 Heritage Festival Community Picnic.
Courtesy of Mike Darnold

The Stroschein House, built in 1927.
Courtesy of Mark Gibson

Rancho Capistrano, north of San Juan Capistrano city limits was sold to Schuller Ministries in the early 1980s.
Courtesy of the San Juan Capistrano Historical Society

Shown here is an aerial view of Capistrano Valley looking northeast.
The mission is center of photo.
Courtesy of the San Juan Capistrano Historical Society

Dr. Norman Neuerburg, called the Michaelangelo of San Juan Capistrano,
personally painted the wall and ceiling decorations in the new Basilica
Church after researching original patterns.
Courtesy of Mike Darnold

*Mission Basilica San Juan Capistrano, the new parish church, was dedicated in 1987
on the corner of Acjachema and Camino Capistrano.
Courtesy of Richard Clinton*

*This view of San Juan Capistrano Regional library from belltower of the Basilica looking northeast.
Courtesy of Mike Darnold*

This aerial view of the northern valley from a hilltop overlooking Marbella Golf and Country Club, is looking northwest with the mission parish church in the center.
Courtesy of Mike Darnold

Shown here is a view looking southwest from
the Basilico belltower in 1989.
Courtesy of Mike Darnold

These are the bells that mysteriously ring by themselves when no one is around, according to legend.
Courtesy of the San Juan Capistrano Historical Society

Bibliography, Articles & Documents

BOOKS

Armor, Samuel, ed. *History of Orange County, Calif.* Los Angeles: Historic Record Co., 1911 and 1921.

Ball, C. D., *Orange County Medical History.* Santa Ana: Flagg, 1926.

Bancroft, Hubert Howe. *California Pastoral, 1796-1848.* San Francisco: A.L. Bancroft, 1888.

___. *History of California.* 7 vols. San Francisco: A. L. Bancroft, 1884-90.

Banks, Homer. *The Story of San Clemente.* San Clemente: El Heraldo de San Clemente, 1930.

Bedford-Jones, Henry. *The Mission and the Man: the Story of San Juan Capistrano.* Pasadena: San Pasqual Press, 1939.

Bell, Horace. *Reminiscences of a Ranger or Early Times in Southern California.* Santa Barbara: Wallace Hubbard, 1927.

Boscana, Geronimo. *Chinigchinich.* Santa Ana: Fine Arts Press, 1933.

Bowers, Stephen. *Orange County, Calif.: History, Soil, Climate, Resources, Advantages.* Board of Trade of Santa Ana, Los Angeles: Los Angeles Printing Company, 1891.

Carillo, Leo (with Ed Ainsworth). *The California I Love.* Englewood Cliffs: Prentice-Hall, 1961.

Chapman, Charles E. *A History of California: The Spanish Period.* New York: McMillan and Co., 1921.

Chappell, William. "St. John of Capistrano." Unpublished Manuscript, San Juan Capistrano Historical Society.

Cleland, Robert Glass. *From Wilderness to Empire: A History of California, 1542-1900.* New York: Knopf, 1944.

___. *The Cattle on a Thousand Hills: Southern California, 1850-1880.* San Marino: Huntington, Library, 1941.

___. *The Irvine Ranch of Orange County, 1910- 1950,* San Marino: Huntington Library, 1952.

Corney, Peter. *Early Voyages in the North Pacific, 1813-1818.* Washington: Ye Galleon Press, 1965.

Costanso, Miguel. *The Portola Expedition of 1769-1770.* Frederick J. Teggert, ed. Berkeley: University of California Press, 1941.

Cramer, Esther R., Keith A. Dixon et al. *A Hundred Years of Yesterdays: A Centennial History of the People of Orange County and Their Communities.* Santa Ana: Orange County Centennial Inc., 1988.

Cunningham, Capt. William. *The Log of the Courier, 1826-1828. Early California Travel Series.* Los Angeles: Glen Dawson, 1958.

Dana, Richard Henry. *Two Years Before the Mast.* New York: Dutton, 1912.

Davis, William Heath. *Seventy-five Years in California.* San Francisco: John Howell, 1929.

Dumke, Glen S. *The Boom of the Eighties in Southern California.* San Marino: Huntington Library 1944.

Engelhardt, Zephyrin. *San Gabriel Mission.* Chicago: Mission Herald Press, 1927.

___. *San Juan Capistrano Mission.* Los Angeles: Standard Printing Co., 1922.

Federal Writers Project. *California: A Guide to the Golden State.* New York: Hastings House, 1939.

Forbes, Mrs. A. S. C. *Mission Tales in the Days of the Dons.* Chicago: A.C. McClary, 1909.

Fox, Clara Mason. *A History of El Toro.* Santa Ana: Public Steno Shop, 1939.

Freidel, Frank. *America in the Twentieth Century.* New York: Alfred A. Knopf, 1966.

Friis, Leo. *At the Bar.* Santa Ana: Friis Pioneer Press, 1980.

___. *Orange County Through Four Centuries.* Santa Ana: Pioneer Press, 1965.

Garrison, *Myrtle. Romance and History of the California Ranchos*. San Francisco: Wagner, 1935.

Grimshaw, Mary Alice. *The History of Orange County, 1769-1889*. Master's Thesis, University of Southern California, Los Angeles, 1937.

Guinn, James Miller. *Historical and Biographical Record of Southern California*. Chicago: Chapman Publishing Co., 1902.

____. *History of California and Extended Histories of Its Southern Coast Counties*. 2 vols. Los Angeles: Historic Record Co. 1907.

____. *Southern California: Its History and Its People*. 2 vols. Los Angeles: Historic Record Co., 1907.

Hallan-Gibson, Pamela. *Ghosts and Legends of San Juan Capistrano*. San Juan Capistrano: Coastline Printers, 1983.

Hart, Don. *A History of Orange County*. Santa Ana: Miles M. Sharon, Santa Ana High School, 1939.

Hill, Merton E. *One Hundred Years of Public Education in Orange County*. Santa Ana; Orange County Schools Office, 1957.

Hoover, Mildred Brooks, Hero and Ethel Rensch. *Historic Spots in California*. Palo Alto, 1966.

Howell, E. L. *Little Chapters about San Juan Capistrano Mission*. Desert Magazine Press, 1949.

Hunt, Rockwell Dennis, and William Sheffield Ament. *Oxcart to Airplane*. Los Angeles, 1929.

James, George Wharton. *In and Out of the Old Missions*. Boston: Little, Brown and Co., 1906.

Janssens, Augustin. *Life and Adventures in California of Don Augustin Janssens*, William H. Ellison and Francis Price, eds. San Marino: Huntington Library, 1953.

Kenneally, Finbar, ed. *The Writings of Fermin Francisco de Lasuen*. 1 vols. Washington: Academy of American Franciscan History, 1965.

Kistler, Jennie. *Tales Tolled by the Mission Bells*. Los Angeles, 1947.

Knowlton, Charles S. *Post Offices of Orange County, California, Past and Present*. Placentia: Placentia Courier, 1947.

Kroeber, Alfred Louis. *Handbook of Indians of California*. Washington: Bureau of American Ethnology, Bulletin 78, 1925.

Lindley, Walter, and J. P. Widney. *California of the South — Its Physical Geography, Climate, Resources, Routes of Travel and Health Records*. New York: D. Appleton and Co., 1888.

Lund, William S. *Orange County: Its Economic Growth 1940-1980*. Stanford Research Institute, Southern California Laboratories, 1959.

McClure, James D. *California Landmarks*. Palo Alto, 1948. McGroarty, John Steven. *Mission Memories*. Los Angeles: Neuner Corp., 1929.

Meadows, Don. *Historic Place Names in Orange County*. Balboa Island: Paisano Press, 1966.

____. *Orange County Under Spain, Mexico and the United States*. Los Angeles: Dawson's Book Shop, 1966.

Morison, Samuel Eliot, and Henry Steele Commager. *Growth of the American Republic*. 5th ed. 2 vols. London: Oxford University Press, 1962.

Moyer, Cecil C. *Historic Ranchos of San Diego*. San Diego, 1969.

Newmark, Harris. *Sixty Years in Southern California, 1853-1913*. New York: Knickerbocker Press, 1916.

Older, Cora Miranda Baggerly. *California Missions and Their Romances*. New York: Tudor Publishing Co., 1916.

Oral History Program, California State University Fullerton. *Community History Project: San Juan Capistrano*. 2 vols. Fullerton, 1976.

Orange County Genealogical Society. *Saddleback Ancestors, Rancho Families of Orange County*. Santa Ana: Aladdin Litho and Art, 1969.

Orange County Historical Commission. *Yesterdays in Orange County.* Orange: Orange County Historical Commission, 1977.

Orange County Historical Society. *Orange Countiana.* Vol. 3. Fullerton: Christian Printing Service, 1982.

Orange County Historical Society. *Orange Countiana,* Vol. 4. "Architecture: A Window on the Past." Richard Voelkel, ed., 1989.

Orange County Historical Society. *Orange County History Series.*
      Vol. 1. Santa Ana: Santa Ana High School and Junior College Press, 1931.

___. *Orange County History Series.* Vol. 2. Santa Ana: Santa Ana High School and Junior College Press, 1932.

___. *Orange County History Series.* Vol. 3. Santa Ana: Santa Ana High School and Junior College Press, 1939.

Osterman, Joe. *Fifty Years in Old El Toro.* Fullerton: Sultana Press, 1982.

O'Sullivan, St. John. *Little Chapters About San Juan Capistrano.* San Juan Capistrano, 1912.

Palou, Francisco. *Historical Memoirs of New California.* 4 vols. Herbert Bolton, ed. Berkeley: University of California Press, 1926.

___. *Life and Apostolic Labors of Venerable Father Junipero Serra,* C. Scott Williams, trans. Pasadena: G. W. James, 1913.

Parker, Charles Edward. *A Manual of Orange County History.* Santa Ana: Orange County Title Company, 1964.

Parker, Charles Edward, and Marilyn Parker. *Orange County: Indians to Industry.* Santa Ana: Orange County Title Co., 1963.

Pico, Pio. *Historical Narrative.* Arthur P. Botello, trans. Glendale: Arthur P. Clark Co., 1973.

Pitt, Leonard. *Decline of the Californios.* Berkeley and Los Angeles: University of California Press, 1970.

Pleasants, Adelina (Brown). History of Orange County, California. Los Angeles: J. R. Finnell and Sons, 1931.

Pourade, Richard F. *The Silver Dons.* San Diego, 1963.

___. *Time of the Bells.* San Diego, 1961.

Quill Pen Club. *Rawhide and Orange Blossoms: Stories and Sketches of Early Orange County.* Santa Ana: Pioneer Press, 1967.

Ramsey, Mabel and Merle. *Pioneer Days of Laguna Beach.* Laguna Beach: Hastie Printers, 1967.

___. *This Was Mission Country,* Orange County, Ca. Laguna Beach: Mission Printing Co., 1973.

Roberts, C. E. *Adobes of Orange County.* U.S. Works Projects Administration, California, Orange County Series, WPA Research Project No. 3105, Santa Ana, 1936-37.

Robinson, Alfred. *Life in California.* Oakland; Biobooks, 1947.

Robinson, W. W. *Land in California: The Story of Mission Lands, Ranchos, Squatters, Mining Claims, R.R. Grants, Landings, Homesteads.* Berkeley and Los Angeles: University of California Press, 1948.

___. *Old Spanish and Mexican Ranches of Orange County.* Los Angeles: Title Insurance and Trust Co., 1950.

Rush, Philip S. *Some Old Ranches and Adobes.* San Diego, 1965.

Saunders, Charles, and St. John O'Sullivan. *Capistrano Nights.* New York: Robert M. McBride, 1930.

Slayton, Robert A., ed. *Proceedings of the Conference of Orange County History.* Conference of Orange County History, 1988.

Sleeper, Jim. *A Grizzly Introduction to the Santa Ana Mountains: A Boys Book of Bear Stories (not for boys).* Trabuco Canyon: California Classics, 1976.

___. *Great Movies Shot in Orange County.* Trabuco Canyon: California Classics, 1980.

____. *Orange County Almanac of Historical Oddities*. 3 vols. Santa Ana: Ocusa Press, 1971, 1974, 1983.

____. *Turn the Rascals Out: The Life and Times of Orange County's Fighting* Editor Dan M. Baker. Trabuco Canyon: California Classics, 1973.

Smith, Bill. *The Capistrano Story*. Orange: John T. McInnis, 1965.

Smith, Vi. *From Jennies to Jets: The Aviation History of Orange County*. Fullerton: Sultana Press, 1974.

Steele, James. *Old California Days*. Chicago: Homewood Publishing Co., 1889.

Stephenson, Shirley. John J. Baumgartner, Jr.: *Reflections of a Scion of the Rancho Santa Margarita*. Oral History Program, California State University, Fullerton, Community History Project, San Juan Capistrano, OH 1657, 1982.

Stephenson, Terry Elmo. *Caminos Viejos*. Santa Ana: Press of the Santa Ana High School and Junior College, 1930.

____. *Shadows of Old Saddleback*. Santa Ana: Fine Arts Press, 1931.

Swanner, Charles Douglas. *Fifty Years a Barrister in Orange County*. Claremont: Fraser Press, 1965.

____. *Santa Ana: A Narrative of Yesterday*. Claremont: Saunders Press, 1953.

____. *The Story of Company L. Santa Ana's Own*. Claremont: Fraser Press, 1958.

____. *Those Were the Days: Recollections of Charles D. Swanner*. Elsinore: Mayhall Print Shop, 1971.

Talbert, Thomas B. *My Sixty Years in California*. Huntington Beach: Huntington Beach News Press, 1952.

Talbert, Thomas. *The Historical Volume and Reference Works: Orange County, California*. 3 vols. Whittier: Historical Publishers, 1963.

Taylor, Ruth Ellen. *Legacy: The Orange County Story*. Santa Ana: The *Register*, 1979.

Walker, Doris. *Dana Point Harbor/Capistrano Bay: Home Port For Romance*. Dana Point: To-the-Point Press, 1981.

Warner, J. J. Judge Benjamin Hayes; and]. P. Widney. *An Historical Sketch of Los Angeles County*. Los Angeles: 0. W. Smith, 1876.

Webb, Edith Buckland. *Indian Life at the Old Missions*. Los Angeles: Warren F. Lewis, 1952.

Wieman, William Wallace. *The Separation and Organization of Orange County*. Publisher Unknown, 1938.

Wilson, John Albert. *Reproduction of Thompson and West's History of Los Angeles County, California*. Berkeley: Howell-North, 1959.

Wolcott, Marjorie Tisdale. *Pioneer Notes from the Diaries of Judge Benjamin Hayes. 1849-1875*. Los Angeles: McBride Printing, 1929.

ARTICLES

Baker, Charles C. "Mexican Land Grants in California." *Historical Society of Southern California Annual Publication* Vol. 9, No. 3: 236-243.

Barrows, Henry D. "Abel Steams." *Historical Society of Southern California Annual Publication* Vol. 4, No. 3: 197-199.

Bedford-Jones, Henry. "Where Swallows Builded." *Overland Monthly* 65 (January 1915).

Billiter, Bill. "Mission's Old Stones to Get New Strength." *Los Angeles Times*, August 10, 1989.

Bowman, J. N. "The Resident Neophytes (Existentes) of the California Missions." *Historical Society of Southern California Quarterly* Vol. 40, No. 2: 138-148. *Coastline Dispatch*, 1931-1966.

DeJean, Louis. "Twenty Years After." *Overland Monthly*, 85, (April 1927).

Dunnivent, Mrs. Dennis. "San Juan Capistrano Cemetery Stones." *Orange County Genealogical Society Quarterly*, June 1968.

Garr, Daniel. "Planning, Politics, Plunder: The Mission and Indian Pueblos of Hispanic California." *Historical Society of Southern California Quarterly* 54 (Winter 1972).

Geiger, Maynard. "New Data on Mission San Juan Capistrano." *Southern California Historical Society Quarterly* 49 (March 1967).

Haas, Jane Glenn. "Santa Margarita: Betting the Ranch." *The Register*. February 3, 1985.

Hallan, Pamela. "San Juan Historic." *Daily Pilot*. January 25, 1975.

Herman, Peter. "C. Russell Cook." *San Clemente Sun Post*, March 19, 1974.

Kelleher, Susan. "Architect Leaves No Stone Undrawn." *Orange County Register*, August 13, 1989.

Killingsworth, James C., pub. *Orange County Illustrated*. Irvine, 1962-1969.

Korber, Dorothy. "Group Takes Time Trip to Sleepy San Juan." *News-Post*. November 30, 1974.

Magalousis, Nicholas M., and Paul M. Martin. "Mission San Juan Capistrano: Preservation and Excavation of a Spanish Colonial Landmark." *Archeology*, May/June, 1981.

Martin, Charles. "Ever Changing California, Land of Startling Contrasts." *National Geographic Magazine* 15 (June 1929).

Morgan, J., and N. Morgan "Orange, A Most California County." *National Geographic* 160 (December 1981): 750-779.

Parker, Charles Edward. "Ranches of Mission San Juan Capistrano." *Orange County Newsmagazine* 9 (February 2, 1965).

Paulson, Wendy. "Past May Curtail Renewal." Los Angeles Times, October 7, 1989.

Santa Ana Blade, 1889.

Santa Ana Register, August 25, 26, 27, 29, 1925; August 6, 1964; February l6, 19, 1965.

Santa Ana Standard, 1889-1898.

Savage, Thomas. "Interviews with Don Juan Forster." *Historical Society of Southern California Quarterly*, September 1970.

Seelye, Howard and Don Smith. "A Century of Politics in Orange County." *Los Angeles Times*, May 21, 1976.

Shepard, Odell. "Corona del Mar to San Juan Capistrano." *Overland Monthly* 65 (January 1915)

Sleeper, ed., *Rancho San Joaquin Gazette*, all vols. Irvine Co, 1968.

Wright, Allen Henry. "San Juan Capistrano." *Overland Monthly* 57 (March 1911).

Yorba, Alfonso. "Old San Juan — Last Stronghold of Spanish California." *Orange County Newsmagazine*, February 1965.

DOCUMENTS

A List of All Persons and Properties Subject to Taxation Situate or Holding in the County of Los Angeles in the Year A.D. 1850. Los Angeles County Hall of Records.

City of San Juan Capistrano. *General Plan*, adopted Dec. 18, 1974.

Mission San Juan Capistrano. *Baptismal, Marriage and Death Records*, 1776-1886.

Orange County Annual Survey. Mark Baldassare, Director. University of California, Irvine, 1982, 1983, 1984.

Padron of Los Angeles, 1836. Los Angeles City Archives

Padron of Los Angeles, 1844. Los Angeles City Archives

Seventh Census of the United States, 1850. Los Angeles County, California.

Yorba, Alfonso, trans. *Notas Califomias of Don Juan Avila*. San Juan Capistrano Historical Society Archives.

Author Biography

Pamela Hallan-Gibson, a fourth generation Orange Countian, became interested in local history while growing up in San Juan Capistrano. She obtained her bachelor's degree in history from the University of California, Riverside, and a master's degree in public administration from California State University, Long Beach.

Her first career was that of journalist. She later became involved in city government and served as Assistant to the City Manager in San Juan Capistrano and City Manager of La Palma. She retired as City Manager of Sonoma after 26 years of public service.

An active preservationist, Hallan-Gibson served for four years on the Orange County Historical Commission, is a life member of the San Juan Capistrano Historical Society, and is past chairman of San Juan Capistrano Walking Tours. She was a charter member of the City's Cultural Heritage Commission and conducted its first historic sites inventory.

In addition, Hallan-Gibson served as president of the Saddleback College Friends of the Library, and was active in many state and national city management organizations. In Sonoma she is a life member of the Sonoma Valley Historical Society, is past president of the Sonoma Plaza Kiwanis, is a member of Sonoma Valley Friends of the Library, the Sonoma Plaza Foundation Board of Directors, and is currently serving on the New Facility Advisory Committee for Sonoma Valley Hospital.

The author of two books about her home town, Dos Cientos Anos en San Juan Capistrano, Ghosts and Legends of San Juan Capistrano, and Two Hundred Years in San Juan Capistrano, she is also author of three books about Orange County — Orange County, The Golden Promise: An Illustrated History of Orange County, A Century of Service: A History of the Orange County Sheriffs Department, and The Bench and the Bar: A Centennial View of Orange County Legal History. She has also contributed to five other books, a documentary film, and several magazines.

She is married, and has two adult children, and lives in Sonoma Valley.

Index

<u>Colophon</u>

This book is set in ITC-Souvenir, a decorative display typeface. Drawn by Ed Benguiat in 1970, the original face came from Morris Fuller Benton in 1914. He brought the design from two of his earlier designs: *Schelter-Antiqua & Schelter-Kursive,* both from the German foundry of Schelter & Giescke.

Having a rounded and informal look, the face evokes a nostalgic feeling of a time gone by. The typestyle comes from the look of souvenir brochures and catalogs for which it is named. This is the International Typeface Corporation version.